RETURN
OF THE
GRIZZLY

RETURN
OF THE
GRIZZLY

Sharing the Range with Yellowstone's Top Predator

CAT URBIGKIT

Skyhorse Publishing

Skyhorse Publishing books may be purchased in bulk at special discounts for sales promotion, corporate gifts, fund-raising, or educational purposes. Special editions can also be created to specifications. For details, contact the Special Sales Department, Skyhorse Publishing, 307 West 36th Street, 11th Floor, New York, NY 10018 or info@ skyhorsepublishing.com.

Skyhorse® and Skyhorse Publishing® are registered trademarks of Skyhorse Publishing, Inc.®, a Delaware corporation.

Visit our website at www.skyhorsepublishing.com.

10 9 8 7 6 5 4 3 2 1

Library of Congress Cataloging-in-Publication Data

Names: Urbigkit, Cat, author.
Title: Return of the grizzly: sharing the range with Yellowstone's top
  predator / Cat Urbigkit.
Description: New York, NY: Skyhorse Publishing, 2018. | Includes
  bibliographical references.
Identifiers: LCCN 2017038435 | ISBN 9781510727472 (hardcover: alk. paper)
Subjects: LCSH: Grizzly bear—Ecology—Yellowstone National Park Region. |
  Grizzly bear—Yellowstone National Park Region—Management. | Wildlife
  recovery—Yellowstone National Park Region. | Wildlife
  depredation—Yellowstone National Park Region. | Human-animal
  relationships—Yellowstone National Park Region.
Classification: LCC QL737.C27 U73 2018 | DDC 599.78409787/5—dc23
LC record available at https://lccn.loc.gov/2017038435

Cover design by Tom Lau
Cover photo credit: Cat Urbigkit

Print ISBN: 978-1-5107-2747-2
Ebook ISBN: 978-1-5107-2748-9

Printed in China

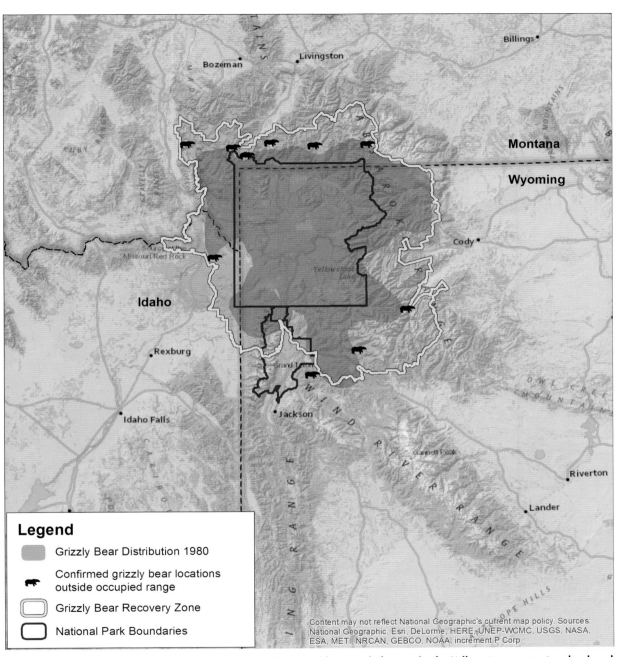

Grizzly bear distribution and confirmed locations outside occupied range in the Yellowstone ecosystem by decade, 1980 to 2010. Maps courtesy of Wyoming Game and Fish Department.

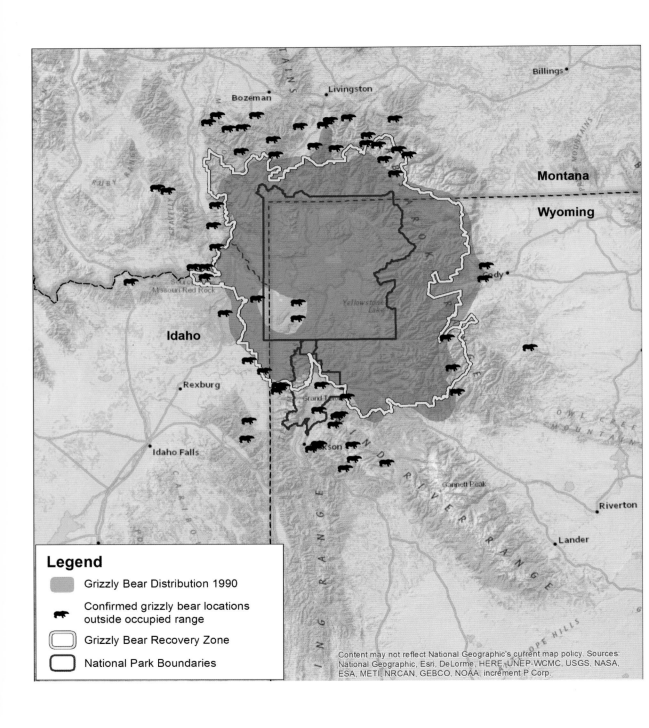

Legend

Grizzly Bear Distribution 1990

Confirmed grizzly bear locations outside occupied range

Grizzly Bear Recovery Zone

National Park Boundaries

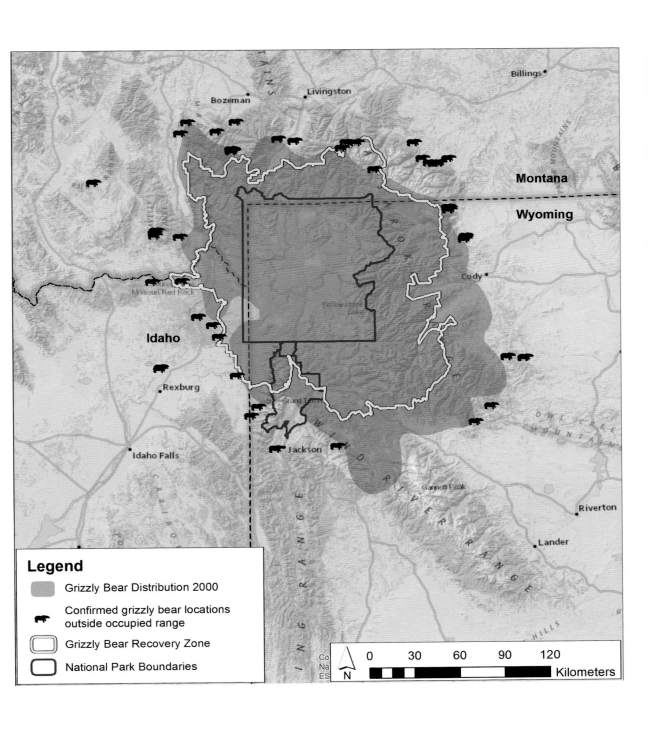

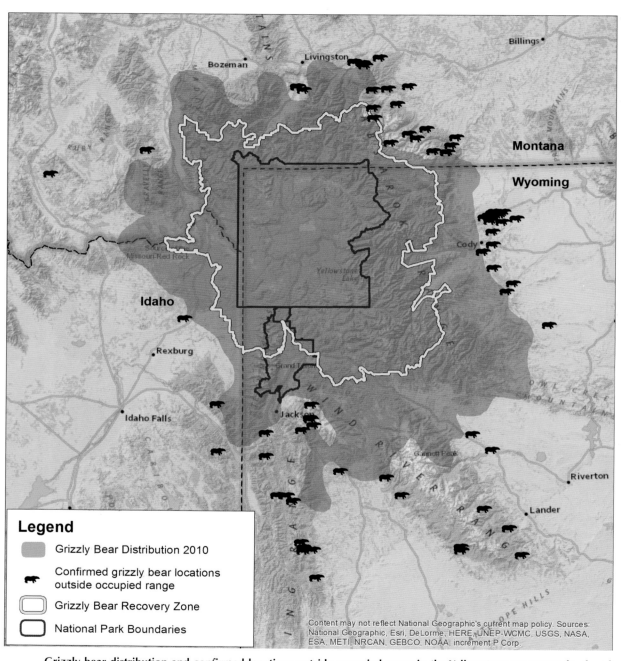

Grizzly bear distribution and confirmed locations outside occupied range in the Yellowstone ecosystem by decade, 1980 to 2010. Maps courtesy of Wyoming Game and Fish Department.

Table of Contents

CHAPTER 1

HUMAN PREY

Yellowstone National Park officials closed the Elephant Back Trail in 2015 after the discovery of human remains.

It took searchers three hours to locate the man's body. When sixty-three-year-old Lance Crosby failed to show up for his 8 a.m. shift at Lake Medical Clinic in Yellowstone National Park on August 7, 2015, park officials were alerted and emergency response teams swung into action. One search and rescue team embarked via boat to check the lakeshore, while others set out on foot to search three trails popular with seasonal workers staying in the nearby government housing area. One searcher hiked up the steep Elephant Back Trail, soon coming upon a grisly scene just off the path: hiking boots protruding from an animal burial mound located on a forested ridge. The ranger backed away and called for an investigative team to respond to the site while he began clearing the area of other human visitors and posting area closure notices. Crosby's remains were located less than a mile from the housing area, along a popular hiking trail rather than a remote wilderness.[1]

As the investigative team approached the site, they saw an adult bear fleeing the burial mound, and heard the sounds of a bear cub or cubs barking and bawling. The victim's body was found in what is called a carnivore burial cache, his remains covered with a mixture of dirt, rocks, grass, and sticks. Caching behavior is typically associated with a large carnivore that covers an animal carcass on which it has fed, and which it intends to return to for further feeding. There are three large carnivores in the Yellowstone region that cache their prey: grizzly bears, black bears, and mountain lions.

Evidence at the scene that hot August day pointed to an adult female grizzly bear with two cubs. An experienced hiker, Lance Crosby had lived and worked in Yellowstone for five seasons, but often hiked alone and without pepper spray to defend himself against an animal attack. Wounds on his body indicated that the victim had fought back but was overtaken by the adult female grizzly that became known to investigators as the Elephant Back female. The mother grizzly and her cubs had partially consumed the man's body at the same location at which he had been killed, probably during the previous afternoon. The bears had rested in daybeds just yards away from the burial cache.

The team collected evidence from the site, and the victim's body was flown out by helicopter. The helicopter returned with two bear traps that were set next to the body burial cache. That night, the 260-pound Elephant Back female grizzly was trapped. In the course of the next few nights, her two cubs were trapped as well. Both were cubs of the year, one weighing forty-one pounds and the other fifty-three pounds.

According to the Board of Review Report on the human fatality: "Due to the DNA evidence linking the Elephant Back female and her cubs to the body burial cache and the consumption of a portion of the body, they were permanently removed from the wild."

The report explained the critical decision made in removal of these federally protected grizzly bears. It stated:

The primary reason these bears were removed from the wild is the killing and consumption of a human. The objective of removing the adult female grizzly bear and two cubs that were involved in the fatal attack and consumption of Mr. Crosby within hours of his death was to prevent these bears from killing and consuming another human in the future.

The bears weren't removed in a retaliatory action for killing a human being, but to prevent these animals from repeating their attacks on another human. They were removed in the interest of human safety.

The adult female grizzly was eventually euthanized and her two cubs were sent to the Toledo Zoo in Ohio, but not before howls of protest over the removal of the bears reverberated around the world.

When news spread that the Elephant Back female had killed a man in Yellowstone National Park, animal advocates raised a rallying cry for this sow grizzly they had nicknamed "Blaze" because of her unique markings. Blaming the human victim for hiking alone and for not carrying bear spray, bear advocates called for the National Park Service to leave the sow grizzly in place. More than 140,000 signatures were attached to a petition stating: "This was a grizzly being a grizzly in grizzly territory. Blaze and her cubs do not deserve

Officials determined that the man had been killed and eaten by a grizzly bear sow and her cubs.

to be killed because someone didn't take necessary steps to avoid a confrontation."

Through social media, calls to save the sow and her cubs quickly spread around the world, and park service officials were flooded with calls and emails. Rob Chaney of the *Billings Gazette* reported that Yellowstone park personnel received hate mail and death threats to the extent that law enforcement officials bumped up efforts to keep park employees and their children safe.

When DNA evidence tied the Elephant Back female to the killing and consumption of a human victim, the Park Service made the decision—following existing policy— to kill the bear. To which the same animal advocates responded with "Superintendent Dan Wenk murdered Blaze today." Marc Bekoff used his *Psychology Today* column to call the death of the bear a "slaughter"

and a "murder." Disregarded in the rhetoric was that the park service took reasonable action by lethally removing a bear that had killed and consumed a human being—an attack that could be repeated by the same animals on another one of Yellowstone's four million annual visitors.

Instead, animal advocates repeatedly noted that a sow grizzly would naturally defend her cubs, that this was "just a bear being a bear." But there is an important distinction in defensive attacks by grizzlies: they usually conclude with the bears fleeing the scene of such an encounter, not eating their victim, as did the Elephant Back female and her cubs.

According to a National Park Service press release on the decision to remove the bears:

Bears are an intelligent, highly adaptable species that quickly learn to exploit new food resources, especially foods that are easily obtained and contain concentrated sources of fat and protein. Since bears readily learn new foods and remember the locations, circumstances, and foods that are available, the possibility of these bears preying on people in the future could not be ruled out.

That possibility wasn't an improbable notion, but was something Yellowstone National Park had experienced just four years prior. In 2011, a sow grizzly bear attacked and killed a man, but park officials viewed it as a surprise attack and decided not to kill the bear. Weeks later and just eight miles from the first fatal attack of the year, the same sow was found feeding on the body of another hiker that had been fatally mauled. With the same bear involved in two human mortalities, park officials made the decision to kill the sow to protect human safety. The agency couldn't risk a repeat offense in 2015.

Crosby's death was the sixth human fatality due to bear attacks in the Yellowstone ecosystem in just five years. This is the reality of human existence in an ecosystem with a thriving grizzly bear population: human fatalities are part of the reality of living with grizzlies. Humans living with grizzlies include human deaths by grizzlies as well.

While arguments about whether grizzly bears in the Yellowstone ecosystem should remain under the protection of the Endangered Species Act rage, there are seven hundred to one thousand grizzly bears roaming the region, most of which occur outside the boundaries of the national parks. Grizzly bears occur across more than 22,000 square miles of the Yellowstone region, in parts of three states, and on private, federal, state, and reservation lands. The great bear has achieved biological recovery goals, and humans inhabiting the Yellowstone region now share the landscape with this monarch of the wild. They live with a species whose Latin name is *Ursus arctos horribilis*. *Horribilis*, as in terrible or horrible—as indeed the species can be when humans become its victims.

In a pilgrimage that has taken place for decades, visitors flock to Yellowstone National Park each year from June through September, expecting to see bears. While most realize that it is illegal to feed the park's wildlife, they do not know the specifics behind policy. Bear management in our national parks changed radically in August 1967 when two teenaged women were killed in separate grizzly bear attacks on the same night in Montana's Glacier National Park. From that night on, NPS officials recognized that bears that fed on garbage in open pits had become a dangerous commodity. The bears had become habituated to the presence of humans, and even worse, associated humans with food, and had become increasingly aggressive in their food-seeking behavior. The National Park Service had to act to prevent further mortalities, and not just in Glacier. Yellowstone officials had also begun debating whether to close its garbage dumps, but the human fatalities in Glacier proved the need for action.

Prior to 1967, Yellowstone's garbage dumps were unfenced pits that were operated from June 1 through mid-September each year (the tourist season), disposing of tons of garbage accumulated by the rising number of visitors to the park over the decades. Five of the park's six major developed areas were eight miles or less from garbage dumps.

Grizzly bears rummaging in the Old Faithful dump. National Park Service photo by R. Robinson.

Congress established Yellowstone National Park in 1872, but hunting had continued in the park for another decade. Once wild animal populations in the park were free from most human persecution, the animals began taking advantage of some of the park's developed areas. Newly constructed hotels were happy to have visiting tourists in these early days of the park and garbage was disposed of in large open pits nearby. Bears—first black bears, but grizzly bears soon followed—learned the pits were food sources, and delighted tourists began gathering nearby to watch as many as two dozen bears forage through human-generated trash each evening. Thus, a tourist attraction was born. By the time the park service began to curtail the public feedings to a single location in Yellowstone in the late 1930s, hundreds of people lined the provided bleacher seating to watch evening feedings that involved up to seventy grizzlies. Eventually the public viewing of bears eating garbage was halted, but the practice of allowing bears to feed in the open dumps away from the public eye continued until the two Glacier National Park human fatalities.

In Paul Schullery's excellent and detailed book *The Bears of Yellowstone* (1986), the author noted that although the park service found it acceptable to allow the bears to feed in the garbage dumps, it did not condone the hand-feeding of bears by park and hotel employees, or visiting tourists. Regardless of park policy, the practice continued and expanded as bears became accustomed to begging food from passing vehicles, with many visitors coming to the park with the specific intent to feed the bears. Schullery

Bears being fed from garbage carts in Yellowstone. National Park Service photo.

writes that by the 1960s, visitors could see as many as thirty black bears begging along the roadsides in Yellowstone. This practice lasted for decades, with the result being nearly fifty human injuries per year, and much property damage.

Park managers learned that some grizzlies traveled long distances to reach the dumps, and some bears entered the park from outside its boundaries for the feeding season. Yellowstone Park's Glen Cole reported in 1971: "The numbers using a dump progressively increased from June to a peak around August 1. Dispersals of bears from concentration sites occurred rapidly after about mid-August and while dumps were still operating."[2]

Reacting to a new management philosophy of national parks as natural areas, the park service eventually cracked down on the hand-feeding of bears, installed bear-proof garbage cans, and closed the last of its garbage dumps to bears in 1970, ending an eighty-year-old supplemental feeding program for the bears. The new philosophy dictated that bears and other wild animals should rely on natural foods within the park's borders, even though the park's elk and bison populations had been kept at low levels through active "ungulate reduction" programs until that practice was also stopped in 1968. The park had been far from "natural" since its inception, and the heavy hand of management was evident across the landscape.

With relatively low numbers of large predators in Yellowstone, park managers had developed programs in the 1930s to

Return of the Grizzly

keep elk and bison populations in check. Yellowstone's ungulate reduction program involved live-trapping elk that were then shipped elsewhere, or were shot by park rangers and butchered. The park disposed of four hundred to four thousand elk in this manner each year. Over about a thirty-year period (1934–1967), the park service killed or removed more than sixty thousand elk. But in its place came what became known as the "firing line"—hunters lined up outside the park's boundary in Montana to kill elk as soon as they stepped out of the park. Public outcry shut this practice down as well in the 1980s.

Within a few years of halting the ungulate reduction program, Yellowstone Park managers grew concerned about elk overpopulating the range and damaging the ecosystem. With the halt of the reduction program, the park's bison population grew from four hundred animals in 1967 to 1,049 in 1975 (a 162 percent increase), while the elk population grew from 4,865 to 12,607 (a 159 percent increase) during the same time period.[3] Although these ungulate populations grew quickly, it would be a few years before Yellowstone's grizzlies began to rely on this food source. The overpopulation of elk was the primary reason eventually cited for the gray wolf reintroduction program that took place in the mid-1990s; it was the park service's method for reducing the elk population. The overwhelming success of the program re-establishing another large predator in Yellowstone eventually became a factor in a population crash for the park's elk population.

Not everyone supported the policy of making bears rely only on natural food sources, as some worried that the bear population could decline in reaction to a drastic reduction in garbage, a key food source. Their concerns were soon justified, when in response to the loss of garbage, Yellowstone bears began ranging more widely. They came into more conflicts with humans, with bear managers killing or relocating many bears deemed to be a problem. The upside was that human injuries by bears decreased to about ten per year, but many bears were destroyed or removed from the population, either by bear managers or private citizens who soon came into contact with these roaming bears outside the park. Bear managers reported that in the two-year period of the late 1960s when Yellowstone was reducing the amount of garbage available at its last dump, an average of fifty-three grizzlies and 119 black bears—all deemed "nuisance" animals—were captured and moved to backcountry areas of the park each year, while an additional nine grizzlies and twenty-six black bears were killed each year. Relocating bears is viewed as a short-term solution, since bears have a high rate of return due to their natural homing abilities.

Grizzly bear researchers Frank and John Craighead had spent a decade (the 1960s) tracking grizzlies in Yellowstone Park, and when they advised against the abrupt closure of the dumps (which they termed "ecocenters," reflecting the importance of this food source), the resulting fallout ended their research in the park in a very public dispute with park officials. As the Craigheads had predicted, the closure of the park's garbage dumps resulted in changes in bear behavior as bears sought out other food sources, got into trouble with humans while doing so, and were relocated or removed from the population. John Craighead maintained that the closure of the dumps resulted in a shocking 50 percent reduction of Yellowstone's grizzly population.[4]

Grizzly bears at the Canyon dump. National Park Service photo by R. Robinson.

Agencies were under much scrutiny and criticism from those concerned about the future of the grizzly in the Yellowstone ecosystem, and with the knowledge gap left with the departure of the Craigheads in 1972, a new unit was formed. The Interagency Grizzly Bear Study Team, created in 1973, was charged with monitoring and researching the Yellowstone ecosystem's grizzlies. It would take a few years for the team to get the necessary infrastructure in place, but in future years these bear researchers would provide much valuable information that would be used for bear management and conservation.

Alarmed about the downward decline of grizzlies, in 1974 the Fund for Animals, Inc. petitioned the US Fish and Wildlife Service (FWS) to list grizzly bears in the contiguous forty-eight states as a species in danger of extinction. When the listing decision was

issued a year later, FWS had decided to list grizzly bears in the lower forty-eight states as a "threatened" species pursuant to the Endangered Species Act.

The grizzly bear listing decision found that grizzlies were threatened due to three factors:[5]

1) Present or threatened destruction, modification, or curtailment of habitat or range.
   (a) The range of the grizzly bear, which at one time was much of the western United States, is now confined to isolated regions in Montana, Idaho and Wyoming.
   (b) Land use practices, including livestock grazing, timbering, and trial construction in areas where these bears still occur

have resulted in the building of numerous access roads and trails into areas which were formerly inaccessible. This has resulted in making the bears more accessible to legal hunters, illegal poachers, human-bear conflicts, and livestock-bear conflicts.

2) Overutilization for commercial, sporting, scientific, or educational purposes. Many persons consider these bears as dangerous vermin; such an attitude results in a continual loss of animals through indiscriminate illegal killing. Other bears are taken regularly in control operations, because they are considered a threat to human safety, and still others are lost because of livestock depredations on public and private lands. In addition, legal sport hunting is continuing in two of the three states where grizzlies still occur. The resulting total mortality is considered excessive both by the Montana Cooperative Wildlife Research Unit and the National Academy of Sciences.

3) Other natural and manmade factors affecting its continued survival.

   a) In two of the three areas where grizzly bears still occur, they are isolated from other populations so that they cannot be reinforced, either genetically or by movement of individual bears.

   b) Increasing human use of Yellowstone and Glacier National Parks, as well as livestock use of surrounding national forests, will exert increasing detrimental pressures on grizzly bears.

   c) Rapid closing of the garbage dumps in Yellowstone National Park in 1970 and 1971 may have resulted in a dispersal of the bears out of the park and into adjacent states where they were and are subject to legal and illegal killing.

At the time grizzlies were placed under federal protection, the Yellowstone region was believed to harbor only 136 grizzly bears. The national park famous for its bears formed the core of a very small grizzly bear population.

Bear managers continued to struggle with the very real and justified public perception that agency action resulted in dire consequences for grizzlies. With the closure of the park's dumps, grizzlies had moved to garbage dumps at the park's gateway communities in Gardiner, West Yellowstone, and Cooke City, Montana until those dumps were closed in the late 1970s, and most conflicts with bears during this time "involved food-conditioned bears aggressively seeking human foods."[6] This program of eliminating food-conditioned bears from the landscape had taken its toll.

The effort to rid the park of bears conditioned to approach human developments for food rewards had worked. Park managers noted that, "by 1979, grizzly and black bears with prior knowledge of sources of unnatural foods within developed areas in the park appeared to be gone from the populations."[7] But the effort had taken more than a decade, and the grizzly bear population had been decimated in the process.

Fortunately, wild grizzlies could be found in more remote regions of the ecosystem, away from most masses of tourists, unnatural foods, and conflicts. Grizzly

Grizzly bears at the Trout Creek dump in Yellowstone National Park, 1964. National Park Service photo by John Good.

bear presence was increasingly documented south of Yellowstone National Park in the late 1970s, in the northern portion of the Bridger-Teton National Forest, especially in the Teton Wilderness, with researchers tallying about forty-five bears in this region, including sows with cubs.[8]

The need for a concerted effort to bring grizzlies back from the brink of extinction resulted in the creation of the Interagency Grizzly Bear Committee (IGBC) in 1983. Consisting of high-level administrative officials from most federal and state agencies involved in grizzly bear management, the IGBC would gain increasing importance in the following years as it worked to ensure grizzly bear recovery and to coordinate policy, planning, management, and research among the multiple jurisdictions represented by the agencies. The committee

structured subcommittees representing each grizzly bear population in the lower forty-eight, including the Yellowstone Ecosystem Subcommittee (YES). YES works closely with the Interagency Grizzly Bear Study Team, the interdisciplinary group of scientists and biologists responsible for long-term monitoring and research efforts on grizzly bears in the Greater Yellowstone ecosystem. While the committee was to lead recovery efforts, the study team was to conduct the necessary research. In 1981, Chris Servheen had been brought on board as the first US Fish and Wildlife Service grizzly bear recovery coordinator, a position he ultimately held for thirty-five years, retiring in the spring of 2016 shortly after his agency announced its intention to remove grizzlies from federal protection.

Finally rid of the garbage dumps and the

Return of the Grizzly

food-conditioned bears, Yellowstone began a new era of grizzly bear management consisting of two primary management actions. The first involved restricting human use in areas with seasonal concentrations of grizzlies. Called "bear management areas," these areas encompass more than 20 percent of the park and are more accurately described as human use restricted areas, since their purpose is to control human use. The second action included minimizing bear–human interactions that could result in human habituation of grizzlies, and to lessen the risk of bear-caused human injuries.

According to Yellowstone park bear manager Kerry Gunther, this era of bear management was characterized by a major change in grizzly bear behavior: while most conflicts in the past had involved food-conditioned bears aggressively seeking human foods, during the next decade most conflicts involved "habituated, but not food-conditioned, bears seeking natural foods within developed areas and along roadsides."[9]

No longer accustomed to receiving foods from a close association with humans and human developments, these bears were simply habituated to the presence of people by their many encounters with park visitors and their vehicles along the roadsides—meetings that did not result in a negative experience for the bears. Habituated bears do not display avoidance behavior around humans or human use areas, in stark contrast to most wild grizzlies that live outside of protected areas and tend to avoid humans. The initial park service response to human-habituated roadside grizzlies was to trap and relocate the bears away from human developments.

Bear managers then questioned if grizzlies could be taught to avoid people and human developments, although Yellow-

stone's grizzlies had learned to live for nearly a century without the need to avoid humans. Park officials teamed up with the Wyoming Game and Fish Department (WG&F) to conduct a series of aversive conditioning experiments designed to condition bears to a new behavior—that of avoiding humans.

Aversive conditioning tests were undertaken from 1986 to 1989, and involved shooting rubber bullets at adult grizzly bears that frequented human developments or campsites in the park. At first, all the bears that were fired upon would flee the scene, generally not returning for a few weeks. As time passed, however, most bears simply fled the scene for a short amount of time before returning. When bears left the aversive conditioning site, they often moved away from the test site to other campsites or areas of human development. All in all, the experiments were not overly successful, with researchers finding that "providing an unpleasant experience to grizzly bears only altered their nuisance behavior temporarily."[10] They added, "Although we were not able to demonstrate a correlation between the bears' behavior and a fear of humans, the general avoidance response exhibited by bears to being hit with a rubber bullet (and possibly relating the experience to a unique sound) suggests that if aversive conditioning is applied often enough and under ideal circumstances, fear could be established in habituated bears."

Or the bears could just get sneakier, as naturalist Olaus J. Murie learned when he tried aversive conditioning on park bears back in the 1940s. He wrote that the bears learned to avoid park-specific personnel and vehicles, but not other people or vehicles.

Still, the researchers recommended aversive conditioning should be considered prior to relocating or destroying nonaggressive bears. Just as Murie had found decades earlier, later park bear managers discovered that the bears seemed to recognize park staff and their vehicles, and appeared to learn the distance from which rubber bullets could be effectively deployed. It was a new generation of bear managers and bears that repeated the lesson in the quest to reduce potential conflicts.

The severity of the potential problem posed by aggressive grizzlies was brought home in June 1983, when a six-hundred-pound adult male grizzly pulled twenty-three-year-old William Roger May of Wisconsin from the tent where he had been sleeping alongside his companion. May was dragged several hundred yards away from the tent and killed. The attack occurred just north of Yellowstone in an established campground in the Gallatin National Forest. Officials euthanized the man-killing bear the following evening.

Unfortunately, one tragedy followed another. The next summer, in July 1984, a twenty-five-year-old woman at a backcountry campsite inside Yellowstone National Park was dragged from her tent by a grizzly, then killed and substantially consumed. The bear that killed her, believed to be an adult male, was never found.

Both of these human fatalities are considered the result of predatory attacks by grizzly bears. The victims were pulled from their tents in the middle of the night by grizzlies that appeared to have viewed these humans as prey, and which then fed on their victim's bodies.

Two years would pass before Yellowstone's next grizzly-caused human mortality, when a photographer was killed after approaching a grizzly bear at close range in Yellowstone's Hayden Valley in 1986.

Thirty-eight-year-old William Tesinsky of Montana was killed by adult female Bear 59, who consumed much of his body before rangers found the bear, who was still feeding on his remains, and killed her.[11] Bear 59 had been a well-known and often-photographed bear, having previously been captured and moved away from areas of human development on numerous occasions—not because of aggressive behavior, but because of her human habituation. Her most recent relocation had taken place just a month prior, and the two cubs that had been at her side at that time were not found again.

The year 1988 would go down as one for the history books in Yellowstone National Park. Yellowstone's policy to let naturally caused wildfires burn was tested in a catastrophic way. That June, a series of eighteen lightning-caused fires were allowed to burn in the park since they were located away from human developments. Officials expected that July rains would quench the fires, but the rains never came. By late July, when the moisture content of vegetation in the park had fallen to just 2 percent, the situation had become so extreme that the Interior Department announced that all fires, regardless of origin, would be fought.

By then Yellowstone had become an inferno. More than fifty wildfires broke out in and around the park, fed by increasing winds and severe drought conditions, and eventually evolving into one catastrophic wildfire complex. Winds picked up burning embers and carried them more than a mile and a half away, sparking new spot fires separate from the main fires. Flames moved across the landscape at more than five to ten miles a day. August 20, 1988, became known as "Black Saturday" as the fires doubled to more than 480,000 acres in size.

The year saw the largest wildfires in Yellowstone's history, and resulted in the closure of the entire park for all non-emergency personnel. The wildfires continued, burning nearly 40 percent of the park, until the snows of mid-September provided relief. More than $120 million was spent fighting these fires, with ten thousand firefighters on the scene at the peak of action—the largest firefighting effort in the nation's history.[12]

As park employees walked through burn areas attempting to survey the number of large animals that had succumbed to the flames, they found hundreds of dead elk, bison, and moose, but no dead predators. What they did find were plenty of live grizzly bears coming to feast on the buffet left by the receding flames.[13]

With the closure of the dumps, bears turned to seeking out natural foods.

CHAPTER 2

BEARS REBOUND

Grizzly bear cub of the year.

He was born in 1990, part of the baby-bear boom that was unleashed in Yellowstone National Park with that spring's den emergence. With only sixteen sows producing thirty cubs the year prior, 1990 brought an abundance of fresh cubs to the park's meadows and hillsides, with twenty-four grizzly sows emerging from their winter dens with fifty-seven cubs at their sides, including three litters of four. It was a great year for the Yellowstone grizzly population.

He was first captured near Mount Washburn in late July 1993, as a three-year-old male. That's when bear managers placed the tag in his ear, identifying the boar as Bear No. 211. He would eventually become one of Yellowstone's most famous bears, spending nearly all his life within the boundaries of the park, often viewed along the park roadsides but never causing problems. By the time he was ten years old, No. 211 had grown to nearly six hundred pounds, and his battle-scarred head proved he ruled his domain. Visitors to the park called him "Scarface" because of the healed wounds on the right side of his face, most likely inflicted during battles with other bears. He was a frequent visitor to the culvert traps set by bear researchers, who laughed in recognition, quickly processed his vital statistics, and set him free once again. In his twenty-five years of living in the park, he was captured seventeen times; one year he was captured three times in one week. When he was captured for the last time in the summer of 2015—in the same area he'd first been captured as a three-year-old—his weight had dropped to 338 pounds, nearly half that of his prime. The old bear wasn't expected to live much longer. In late November 2015, Scarface was shot and killed just outside the park in the Gallatin National Forest by an elk hunter who claimed he shot in self-defense

While most bear watchers had expected Scarface would meet his end by entering his winter den and simply not emerging from it in the spring, or perhaps in a brutal conflict with a bigger bear or a pack of wolves, no one anticipated the old boar would be shot. The bear had lived a full life in Yellowstone: during his time, Yellowstone's grizzly population doubled, wolves were introduced and thrived, and the elk population crashed. He'd experienced drought and deep snows, produced offspring that still continue his lineage, and thrilled thousands of visitors who encountered him each year. Scarface serves as an example of the resiliency of grizzly bears in the Yellowstone region, and in the effectiveness of a changing bear management philosophy.

After the setbacks to Yellowstone's grizzly bear population resulting from the closure of the dumps and the effort to remove food-conditioned bears, park officials had grown weary of their rather unsuccessful attempts to keep bears away from people. In 1990, the National Park Service changed its grizzly bear management program in Yellowstone National Park. Instead of putting so much effort towards hazing or relocating bears away from roadsides, it instead would concentrate on managing the people who stopped to view these bears. The policy worked well for decades, but eventually would cause controversy between bear managers far down the road of grizzly recovery.

The Yellowstone grizzly population began rebounding in the 1980s. According to bear researchers, "The turning point appeared to occur in the mid-1980s, when the policy of preventing adult female mortalities whenever possible began to be widely observed."[14]

The grizzly bear is one of the largest predators on the western landscape, but its biology sets the stage for slow gains in population growth. Most sow grizzlies do not give birth for the first time until they are six years old. They have an average of two cubs per litter, and don't reproduce again for another three years. Added together, these characteristics mark the grizzly bear as having one of the slowest reproductive rates amongst mammals. Most grizzly sows stop reproducing in their mid- to late-twenties.

The expansion of a grizzly population into new range is a slow process as well. Young females often establish home ranges overlapping their mother's home range, so population dispersal across a landscape is gradual and is usually initiated by young male grizzlies that tend to range much more widely than females.

From 1983 through 2001, the Yellowstone region's grizzly bear population grew at an average annual rate of 4 to 7 percent, with the population expanding their range beyond the park's borders.[15]

The grizzly's slow reproductive rate makes for slow population growth.

Bear managers outside Yellowstone National Park were soon dealing with grizzly population success, as the population grew past the park's boundaries and expanded not just to areas adjacent, but outside the official grizzly bear recovery zone as well.

The first grizzly-killed beef calves were confirmed on Paul Walton's Blackrock grazing allotment some thirty miles south of Yellowstone in 1992, when six calves were killed.[16] The next year, his calf losses increased from 2.7 percent of his eight-hundred-head herd to 12.4 percent, with twenty-five confirmed kills by grizzlies. Researchers found a consistent pattern to the kills—they took place at night, with a kill occurring every third night. Adult male grizzlies conducted most kills, with three males responsible for 90 percent of confirmed kills. One of the male bears identified as a habitual offender was subsequently shot and killed after behaving aggressively toward a hunter. Another was relocated away from the area twice, but kept returning to kill cattle before being removed from the population. The third repeat offender left the area after two nights of aversive conditioning by bear managers, but returned to kill cattle the next year.

The researchers noted:

We believe grizzly bears were in the early- to mid-stage of re-establishment on the Blackrock area during our study. The Blackrock grizzly bear population was dominated by adult and sub-adult males, and although females were present, it was not until 1994–96 that we captured females with young.

Return of the Grizzly

Also, grizzly bears were only seasonal residents on the study area until one denned there in 1996.[17]

The researchers concluded that removal of adult male habitual offenders should have minimal impact on the grizzly population while still being effective in decreasing depredations on livestock. They added: "Cattle owners should not be expected to endure excessive losses or abandon all areas inhabited by grizzly bears. This only heightens animosity toward bears and erodes support for population recovery."

The grizzly bear research project on the Blackrock allotment ended in 1996, and Paul Walton passed away two years later. Although the ranch continued to operate, cattle were removed from the allotment in 1999, and the family eventually agreed to a buyout of the allotments so the area could be permanently closed to livestock grazing. This was a cause for celebration in the conservation community.[18]

Neighboring livestock producers to the south feared their allotments would be targeted next. They had plenty of reason. The Bridger-Teton National Forest had already publicly discussed its desire to eliminate the four remaining domestic sheep allotments in the Upper Green area of the forest, and neighboring cattlemen in the Upper Green had their first confirmed grizzly bear calf kills in 1993. What had started as a trickle of grizzly problems in the Upper Green—dozens of miles outside the grizzly bear recovery zone—became an open floodgate.

The 1990s were contentious for livestock producers in the Yellowstone region. United States Interior Secretary Bruce Babbitt's proposed Rangeland Reform initiative was viewed as an assault on public lands

Initiation of grizzly bear range expansion usually occurs when young male bears roam into new territory.

livestock grazing; wolf reintroduction to Yellowstone National Park and Central Idaho was taking place; and entire cattle herds in western Wyoming were tested and slaughtered by federal animal health officials after contracting the highly contagious disease brucellosis from infected elk that share the same rangeland. Further, in an interagency effort to keep bison from spreading brucellosis to Montana's cattle herds, Yellowstone officials were capturing and killing thousands of bison as the animals left the park and entered Montana. Bison activists blamed the slaughter on ranchers, even though brucellosis had been subject to a national disease eradication campaign since the 1930s. Brucellosis is classified by the CDC both as a human health hazard as well as a potential agent of biological terrorism. Livestock producers felt they were in the crosshairs of a hostile public that had been little informed of the complexities of these issues.

Although the first federal grizzly bear recovery plan was adopted in 1982, the plan was amended in 1993 to delineate the official recovery zone where grizzlies and grizzly habitat would be managed to achieve bear recovery, and within which bear population parameters would be monitored. Meanwhile, grizzly bear depredations on livestock grazing far outside the bear recovery zone continued to escalate, with 135 of Bill Thoman's domestic sheep

Biologists have immobilized a bear and prepare to lift it out of the trap and onto the tarp for data collection. USGS photo Interagency Grizzly Bear Study Team.

Return of the Grizzly

killed by bears in the Upper Green in one summer grazing season. While thirty-one of the kills could be definitively attributed to grizzly bears, black bears were also involved in many depredations. Six black bears were killed in attempt to stop the depredations, and four grizzlies were captured in the area and relocated to Yellowstone National Park or areas adjacent to the park. Bears were also preying on beef cattle in the Upper Green, killing three yearlings and thirteen calves. Grizzlies were making their appearance known in areas of the Yellowstone ecosystem where they hadn't been confirmed for decades, and that in itself presented challenges across the multiple jurisdictions and wide array of land managers and users of lands in the region.

In Yellowstone National Park, humans are temporary visitors and human activity is tightly controlled or prohibited in response to grizzly bear presence. But the moment grizzlies exited the park, they entered a landscape inhabited by humans year-round, with residences and other human developments, such as agriculture, industry, and roads, as well as the wide array of human activities that make up everyday life. In these areas, the landscape could be shared with grizzlies, but not managed primarily for the benefit of the bear. Conflicts were inevitable, and dealing with those conflicts became a significant focus of bear managers.

When it came to managing problem bears, the tactics used in the Yellowstone region were the same as those eventually adopted by many bear managers around the world. Interagency Grizzly Bear Guidelines defined a nuisance bear as one:

- that causes significant depredation to lawfully present livestock or uses

unnatural foods which had been reasonably secured from the bear, "resulting in conditioning of the bear or significant loss of property"; or

- that has displayed aggressive (not defensive) behavior toward humans, constituting a demonstrable immediate or potential threat to human safety; or

- that had an encounter with a human that results in substantial human injury or loss of human life.[19]

Bears that show unnatural aggression (predatory behavior) toward humans or that cause severe human injury or death, were to be removed from the population, either through killing or placing the animals in permanent captivity.

Bears that show natural aggression (such as defense of young or food, during a surprise encounter, or self-defense) are generally not removed from the population, even if the aggression results in human injury or death, unless the particular circumstances warrant removal.

Live capturing bears at conflict locations and relocating them to remote locations away from the source of conflict is a common practice for nonaggressive grizzlies that are food conditioned or human habituated. Under the federal guidelines, nonaggressive bears were to be relocated at least once before they could be permanently removed from the population.

There are a number of reasons for relocation of non-aggressive bears involved in conflicts, since relocation:

- reduces the probability of property or livestock damage, or human interactions in areas where the potential for conflict is high;

After repeated livestock depredations, adult male grizzlies are captured and relocated away from livestock.

- reduces the potential for bears to become food conditioned;
- allows bears the opportunity to forage on natural foods and remain wary of people; and
- may prevent removing bears from the population.

Agencies in the Yellowstone region were strictly adhering to the guidelines, but they were spending a lot of time moving grizzlies around, and soon they were having a difficult time trying to find places that were willing to receive the bears. Yellowstone

had been willing to accept grizzlies that were involved in livestock killing (since the park had no livestock) but were unwilling to accept bears that had been in conflicts with humans or human foods. But the park had enough of its own bears to deal with, and really didn't want to accept any more bears from the outside.

Reg Rothwell of the Wyoming Game and Fish Department addressed the Yellowstone Ecosystem Subcommittee in 1996, asking, "The recovery area is full, or pretty close to full. Where can we move bears that are outside the recovery area?"

Rothwell asked the committee to help find areas outside of the park, but still within the grizzly bear recovery zone, where agencies could relocate bears out of conflict areas that were outside the recovery zone.

"We are going to be facing this more and more," he said. "If the expansion continues, if we need to get more bears out of these truly multiple-use areas, I see increasing numbers of bear removals from the population."

Realizing that one way to reduce conflicts and keep from having nuisance bears in areas of grizzly population expansion, the committee began discussions of expanding its food storage and sanitation guidelines across the range where grizzlies were newly occurring. Keeping human foods, game carcasses, livestock and pet feed, and garbage away from bears was key to preventing conflicts, and strict food storage orders already existed in areas such as Yellowstone National Park and adjacent areas. Perhaps those orders should be expanded across a much wider range, Rothwell suggested.

"In the last few years we had enough instances in the Wind Rivers, down to the Big Sandy, with black bears," Rothwell said. "We should be looking at food storage regulations, whatever, for bears in general." But the agencies preferred to educate the public about the importance of proper food storage, and encouraged a voluntary approach rather than a regulatory one for the immediate future.

With all the activities undertaken by the multiple agencies in the region to deal with the expanding grizzly population, bear managers questioned whether the Yellowstone region might be reaching its grizzly bear carrying capacity. Lee Eberhardt and Richard Knight, two members of the Interagency Grizzly Bear Study Team, set about answering that question in a paper published in the *Journal for Wildlife Management*.[20] Using data from 1990–94 on the minimum number of adult females present (obtained through radio telemetry) combined with estimates of population composition, the pair estimated the minimum Yellowstone grizzly population was 245 bears, with a total population estimate of 390 bears.

"Current population size appears to be approaching a level where management to curb further increases might be desirable, even though it will be highly controversial," explained Eberhardt and Knight. While the grizzly population was increasing, so was human use of grizzly bear range, increasing the potential for human-bear conflicts. They warned that, "Relaxation of concerns about population size and trend probably will lead to an increase in bear mortalities, because it is much easier to destroy a bear than to manage sources of bear-human conflicts." And the researchers further cautioned: "a few percentage points of adult survival separate an increasing from a decreasing population, so that the population could easily slide back to a decreasing trend."

Eberhardt and Knight warned that the Yellowstone grizzly population may be approaching carrying capacity, and suggested that the Wyoming Game and Fish Department's interest in eventually hunting grizzlies "needs to be considered as a management effort, because removal of some males may reduce competition for resources." They continued that "because bear-human conflict situations continue to increase and often result in the death of bears, we believe alternate use of some bears is worthwhile."

The pair noted strong objections to any grizzly bear harvest should be expected from those wishing to keep grizzlies in a "natural" state, and countered, "The only apparent way to do that is to remove people from grizzly range."

The key issues raised in the Eberhardt and Knight paper would be subject to debate for decades to come, including the size of the population, whether the population had reached its carrying capacity, and the removal of bears from the population. Regardless, the US Fish and Wildlife Service (FWS) set about updating the official Grizzly Bear Recovery Plan to reflect current scientific knowledge. When the updated plan was released for public review, the agency received a few thousand comments before adopting the final plan later in the year.

The revised recovery plan was approved by FWS in September 1993. Because of the difficulty in determining the total population number of this secretive, wide-ranging predator, the plan did not call for a target of a specific number of bears to indicate recovered status. Instead the plan called for the monitoring of several population parameters (or criteria) as indicators of population status. The parameters were to be figured on either three-year or six-year averages, reflecting the three-year reproductive cycle for adult females. The plan defined a recovered grizzly bear population as one that could sustain existing human-caused mortality and was well distributed throughout the Yellowstone ecosystem.

The reproduction goal for grizzlies in the 9,500-square-mile Yellowstone recovery area was a minimum six-year average of fifteen females with cubs of the year. In 1996 researchers counted thirty-three females with seventy cubs, for a six-year average of twenty-three females, meeting this recovery goal. According to the Interagency Grizzly Bear Study Team data, this average had steadily increased in the previous twenty years. During the 1970s, the six-year average was twelve females with cubs, and during 1986 to 1993 the average was twenty-one females with cubs.

For the grizzly population to reach recovery goals, sixteen of the eighteen Bear Management Units (BMUs) in the Yellowstone ecosystem must be occupied by females with young. In 1996, researchers found all eighteen BMUs occupied by these family groups. The six-year average was fourteen of the eighteen BMUs occupied, falling a little short of the recovery goal. But officials predicted that if family groups remain distributed in all eighteen BMUs during the next two years, this recovery goal would be achieved.

The Yellowstone mortality target required known man-caused mortality not to exceed 4 percent of the population estimate. No more than three percent of the four-percent limit could be adult female mortalities. The mortality limits are figured on a three-year average, and the limit cannot be exceeded during any two consecutive years for recovery to be achieved. In 1996, there were nine man-caused mortalities, two of which were females. The minimum population estimate was 211 bears. Based on that estimate, the mortality limit was eight bears, of which females could be no more than two. Since human-caused mortalities exceeded the limits, this recovery goal had not yet been achieved.

After the final recovery plan was released in September 1993, twenty environmental groups, led by the Fund for Animals and the National Audubon Society and represented by the Sierra Club Legal Defense Fund (which later changed its name to Earthjustice), filed a lawsuit asserting that the recovery plan was actually a "road map for the bears' forced march to extinction."[21]

A federal court eventually upheld parts of the plan, but found it lacking in addressing bear habitat needs and historic loss of habitat. Rather than appeal the decision, FWS reached a settlement with the groups, agreeing to address habitat-based recovery criteria and the methods used to measure the status of bear populations before the agency would move forward with removing grizzlies from the list of federally protected species. As a result of the lawsuit and settlement agreement, beginning in 2000, the Interagency Grizzly Bear Study Team began a comprehensive evaluation of the demographic data and the methodology used to both estimate population size and establish the sustainable level of mortality for grizzly bears in the Yellowstone ecosystem.

While the biologists and lawyers studied and argued over data and methodology, the general public was not able to learn many bears does it take to reach recovery, and how close to recovery were the Yellowstone bears.

"Things are going darn well with grizzly bear recovery in Yellowstone, there isn't any question about that," Bridger-Teton National Forest Supervisor Thomas Puchlerz told a congregation of western

Proper food storage proved key to reducing conflicts between bears and humans.

Wyoming county commissioners in the fall of 1997. "With recovery we have to deal with success. We are having success."

With occupied grizzly bear range continuing to expand to the south and east of Yellowstone and bears ranging far outside the recovery zone, Puchlerz noted: "Sanitation and human safety is a big issue. It's something we've got to face here, outside the recovery zone. We can't just let people come in and decide to camp without getting them the proper information."

Puchlerz said it was time for people living in bear country to consider the impact of routine actions, such as putting suet (which bears love) out for birds, how they dispose of garbage, and the danger of leaving food in tents and in camps.

"People have got to be aware," Puchlerz said. "We've got a lot of bears out there and

we're going to have to start modifying our behavior. The outfitters are doing an outstanding job . . . That has to move to the general public."

Hunting outfitters throughout the region were already equipping their camps with dogs to keep bears at bay, and encasing their camps in solar-powered electric fencing to keep occupants safe.

The Forest Service was considering instituting food storage regulations throughout the Bridger-Teton National Forest. The regulations had already been in place for a number of years on the northern portion of the forest, but with the increased likelihood of bears obtaining food rewards in other areas, an expansion of the regulations was proposed.

By the time the Yellowstone Ecosystem Subcommittee met later in the fall of 1997, there had been nine human-caused grizzly bear mortalities that year, with five of these grizzlies shot by hunters within a ten-day period on the Bridger-Teton National Forest. Representatives of the Wyoming Game and Fish briefly debated whether to implement an emergency regulation requiring hunters to carry bear spray, but opted to increase its educational efforts instead. While there were few human-grizzly bear conflicts outside the official grizzly recovery zone in 1990, by the end of the decade, conflicts had escalated, and most occurred outside the recovery zone.

The seriousness of expanded grizzly bear presence became apparent in the small northwestern Wyoming town of Wapiti. In 2001, seven grizzly bears were removed from the valley because of their proximity to humans, including three grizzlies that were captured near the school. A ten-foot tall fence was erected around the schoolyard to keep bears out and the children safe.

A tall fence was constructed around the school grounds at Wapiti because of the presence of grizzly bears.

CHAPTER 3

THE UPPER GREEN

The Upper Green's Squaretop Mountain is one of the most scenic landmarks.

Grizzly bears had been gone so long from the Upper Green that few cowboys could remember the stories their ancestors told of the great grizzled bear. Every spring for the last century, ranch families throughout the valley worked from horseback to gather their cattle from the desert sagebrush lowlands and slowly pushed the herds north nearly sixty miles along the Green River Drift Trail. When they arrive in the lush mountain pastures of the Upper Green River region of the Bridger-Teton National Forest, the herds are combined to spend the summer and fall in the largest grazing allotment of the national forest system. The number varies, but nearly six-thousand-head of range cattle make the journey to graze the Upper Green each year.

They arrive to a stunningly beautiful landscape, where dark forests of pine, spruce, and fir give way to grass-covered parks dissected by small trout streams, their banks lined with red-barked willows. High-elevation lakes sprinkled with lily pads nestle beneath knolls blanketed with yellow balsamroot, flanked by stands of quaking aspen. The trilling call of a sandhill crane rolls across calm waters in spring, while the sharp bugle of bull elk in rut reverberates through fall mountain mornings. Jagged granite peaks and glaciers of the Wind River Mountains tower above this headwater of the Green River. Escaping the lake, the current builds as it is carried away from the mountains, gaining strength to emerge downstream as the mighty Colorado River that traverses more than seven hundred miles through the American West.

The Upper Green lies some thirty miles north of the small western town of Pinedale, Wyoming. Functioning as the Sublette County seat in a region that has far more cattle than people, the town of two thousand is positioned at an elevation of seven thousand feet amid a broad valley bordered by mountains on three sides, its southern reaches seamlessly giving way to the welcoming sagebrush steppe. Still dusted with traditional western culture, Pinedale has grown to embrace its fame as a mecca for outdoor enthusiasts, its main street dotted with works of both contemporary and western art, and Border Collies rest in the beds of mud-covered ranch trucks parked alongside Subarus adorned with ski racks and kayaks at the local watering hole or coffee shop.

Pinedale and its Upper Green are located in the southern portion of the Greater Yellowstone Ecosystem, its remote wildlands connected by a chain of mountainous terrain that form the Rocky Mountains. Some hundred miles to the north, Yellowstone National Park serves as the nucleus of the ecosystem, and is the place from which grizzly bear recovery would radiate. Yellowstone would serve as the source population that would eventually give the Upper Green its grizzly bears, and a few years later, its wolves.

For the cattlemen in the Upper Green, 1993 marked the year of change. A cowboy had discovered a calf that had been killed by a larger predator than anyone had encountered in the recent past. When a similar kill was found the next summer, federal wildlife officials were called in and confirmed that a grizzly bear had made its presence known. Within a couple of years, there were four grizzlies preying on cattle. The numbers continued to rise.

In 2010, a federal wildlife specialist was sent into the backcountry of the Upper Green to try to capture an injured wolf. His crew members flew overhead in a fixed-wing airplane, trying to pick up the signal from the wolf's radio collar. As he hiked along an old logging road, the radio cracked

on his hip: "You've got to get out of there. There's a line of grizzly bears coming down the trail."

Grizzly bears were coming to the arriving cattle, moving towards the food source as they would to a stream of spawning salmon. By 2015, there were an estimated sixty grizzly bears living in the Upper Green—the largest density of cattle and bears on the continent. By then, the recovery program for Yellowstone's grizzly bears had become an international story of conservation success that still managed to generate controversy, but its impacts had changed the lives of people who live and work in the Upper Green, far outside the official grizzly bear recovery zone.

HELP WANTED: Range rider in mountains. Involves fencing, moving cattle to prevent overgrazing, helping other range riders. Area highly populated with bears and wolves, expect close encounters. Location very remote in the Upper Green in western Wyoming. Cabin provided with propane heat and light, no electricity, no indoor plumbing. Need own horses. Need experience with cattle. Start June 1, end Oct. 31. Call Al-

An advertisement seeking range riders to work in the Upper Green.

Cattlemen in the Upper Green were aware of the grizzly bear problems with cattle on Paul Walton's Blackrock allotment, so it was no great surprise when grizzlies moved further south from Blackrock and entered the Upper Green allotments.

After agency officials were able to confirm that a grizzly bear had killed eleven calves and at least eleven sheep in the Upper Green in July 1997, an adult male grizzly was captured and relocated to the northern portion of Yellowstone National Park.[22] Another grizzly had repeatedly stolen the bait used in bear traps, and managed to trip leg snares without getting caught. Although wildlife officials hoped they had captured the problem bear, ranchers took a "wait and see approach," believing another bear was responsible for the damage. Their cautious approach would serve them well, as they would learn the next summer when the same killing pattern was repeated by the same bear.

Under federal nuisance grizzly bear guidelines, male bears caught depredating on livestock outside the recovery zone could be removed after their second offense.

Females, which are biologically more important for the population, were to be given three strikes. But there were many more livestock missing than in the past.

"What changed the game was in 1997 when we had a significant loss, and we didn't feel like the compensation was adequate," said Upper Green River Cattle Association President Albert Sommers. A lifelong rancher, his family had long produced quality Hereford cattle since homesteading the ranch outside of Pinedale in 1907. Intelligent and articulate, the fifty-eight-year-old state legislator speaks with a gravelly voice and is an ideal spokesman for the concerns of a community in which lives have been altered by the presence of grizzly bears.

The cattlemen found that their numbers simply didn't add up—there were far more calves missing at the end of the grazing season than could be accounted for in the tally

Upper Green River Cattle Association President Albert Sommers.

The Upper Green

The difficulty of finding and confirming livestock killed by grizzly bears was soon evident.

of confirmed kills by grizzlies. They suspected more calves had been killed by grizzlies than could be found and confirmed. Under state statute, the Wyoming Game and Fish Department (WG&F) was required to provide compensation for damages inflicted by trophy game animals, including grizzly bears—even though the species remained under federal protection.

After the grazing season, members of the Upper Green River Cattle Association attended a Wyoming Game and Fish Commission meeting to contest the WG&F's proposed compensation payments for damages to grizzly bears.[23] Prior to 1997, WG&F compensated livestock producers only for confirmed grizzly bear depredations. In 1997, WG&F recognized that more calves were killed by grizzly bears than were found, and adopted a compensation

factor that incorporated these unconfirmed losses. WG&F had set compensation rates based on the three-year study of bear depredations in the Blackrock/Spread Creek allotments near Togwotee Pass, north of the Upper Green. Under the program, WG&F would pay for verified calf losses at the rate of 1.35 calves for every calf known to be killed by grizzlies when cattle are slain in an open range situation and there are more calves missing at the end of the season (in addition to the verified kills). If no additional calves were missing, WG&F would only pay for verified losses at the rate of 1:1, as it did for adult cattle.

The cattlemen argued that the Blackrock allotment was substantially different than the Upper Green. While eight hundred cattle grazed the Blackrock, under the supervision of two range riders, WG&F was able to

Return of the Grizzly

At the end of the grazing season, cattlemen sort members of their herds out of the mixed bunch, and trail them home.

verify that 35.7 percent of the calves known to be dead from all causes were killed by grizzlies. In contrast, the Upper Green had closer to seven thousand cattle grazing, which would have required eighteen riders to document the same percentage of damage as on the Blackrock, but only used five riders at that time. After reviewing information indicating that historic losses had doubled or tripled for some producers in the Upper Green, the WG&F Commission agreed to restructure its compensation formula, and upped the compensation offer to the producers suffering losses. It wasn't all the cattlemen had wanted, but it was better than before. Over the following years, WG&F adjusted the compensation factor based on loss data supplied by Upper Green cattle producers. The cattlemen had taken

a scientific approach to the situation, even publishing a paper about livestock losses to large carnivores in a scientific journal, and their numbers were solid.

Because grizzlies are listed as a threatened species, federal agencies are required to evaluate the environmental impact of various activities on the bear's continued chances for survival. A biological assessment prepared by the Pinedale Ranger District of the Bridger-Teton National Forest in September 1997 determined that continued livestock grazing in the Upper Green "may affect, and is likely to adversely affect the threatened grizzly bear." This finding led the Forest Service to attach a new condition on grazing permits in the Upper Green that would allow the agency to cancel grazing permits to avoid conflicts with grizzlies.

Wyoming Game and Fish Department bear personnel prepare to process a grizzly bear held in a trap after killing cattle in the Upper Green.

The assessment stated: "In 1996, at least eight different bears were documented . . . Given the older ages (five to nine years old) of the four grizzlies trapped and relocated, we suspect grizzlies have been here for a number of years but have gone more or less undetected.

"Male grizzlies previously captured and relocated back into the recovery zone are expected to return and continue predation on sheep and possibly cattle. If Interagency Grizzly Bear Committee recommendations for nuisance bears are followed, these repeat offenders should be removed from the population. In addition, as the Yellowstone bear population expands, other bears may utilize the area or be affected by livestock operations. These bears could be subject to harassment, trapping, human/

bear conflicts, and/or possible accidental handling death.

"We expect documented grizzly use on the district to increase. We also expect increasing use by the public." The assessment continued: "Conservation measures . . . should reduce the possibility of human/ bear conflicts and bear predation on livestock. Bears, however, are bears, and their distribution and use of an area can vary substantially from year to year."

In an interview with a local newspaper, Bridger-Teton Pinedale District Ranger Bob Reese said the Upper Green had become somewhat of a guinea pig for dealing with how to manage a federally protected species when it conflicts with other uses outside its designated recovery zone.[24]

Reese said the result of the biological

Return of the Grizzly

assessment would be requirements that were added to the annual operating plans for the livestock grazing permittees in the Elk Ridge, Upper Green, and Roaring Fork areas. These conservation measures include: immediate reporting of predation; a clause which holds the federal government "harmless from all claims . . . for any damage to life or property (including livestock) arising from . . . encounters with grizzly bears"; all livestock carcasses must be removed or destroyed as soon as possible; sick or injured animals must be treated and/or removed from the forest; and permittees must have clean camps, with food "stored, handled, and disposed of in such a manner as to make it totally unavailable to bears."

One other clause stated, "The authorized Forest officer may order immediate modification or cancellation of any activities authorized by this permit . . . to prevent confrontation/conflict between humans and grizzly bears . . . (or because of) intentional/negligent acts by the permittee or their agents that result in injury or death of a grizzly bear."

In effect, the Forest Service could cancel the grazing permit to avoid conflicts with grizzlies. Reese said: "Basically, for the short term, we will try to manage both cattle and sheep as they are, where they are. For our long-term strategy, we don't have any plans to move cattle out of the cattle allotments. In the long term, if we can find a place where Bill Thoman is willing to go to, we'll move the sheep," and eliminate the domestic sheep grazing allotments in the area.

Thoman expressed opposition to the idea. "If they move my livestock out of there, they'll be coming down on the cattle," he said. "It won't relieve the situation at all. I think it is better, in the overall picture, that there is more than one class of livestock there."

Thoman added that the problem was that grizzly managers "have an overflow of their product, and they don't know what to do with it."

Reese said he was unsure what the future would hold in terms of grizzly bear management on the district. "But I don't think we can keep trapping and moving bears back to Yellowstone. Delisting won't really resolve it either. We've got more questions than answers right now."

The Grizzly Bear Recovery Plan stated: "It is recognized that grizzly bears occasionally will move and even reside permanently in areas outside recovery zones. Bears can and are expected to exist outside recovery zone lines in many areas. However, only the area within the recovery zone will be managed primarily for grizzly habitat."

United States Fish and Wildlife Service (FWS) Grizzly Bear Recovery Coordinator Chris Servheen had a different view than the Bridger-Teton's Bob Reese. When asked in an interview at the time whether grizzly bears should take priority over other uses of the Upper Green, Servheen replied, "No. But the issue is complex." Servheen added that land management agencies needed to "balance the needs of local people with the needs of the bear." He said while grizzly bears outside the recovery zone aren't to receive top priority over other uses, "bears are still protected," and the agencies need to "minimize conflicts with bears on public lands."

Servheen said the bear recovery plan "didn't anticipate" grizzlies being present and causing problems in the area north of Pinedale. The recovery plan was written to guide management within the recovery zone, and imposed human-caused mortality limits as one of three criteria to measure recovery. Serveheen also noted that if grizzly mortalities occurred beyond ten miles of the recovery zone, the bear deaths would not count against the mortality criteria. According to the recovery plan, the recovery zone is defined as the area with the needed habitat to support a recovered grizzly population, and is the area where the recovery criteria are to be measured—not outside that zone.

According to the recovery plan, bears outside the recovery zone that are involved in conflicts are to be captured and relocated to a location within the recovery zone, or removed from the population. "Capture and removal of nuisance bears outside the recovery zone by authorized agency actions is necessarily more lenient than within the recovery zone."

To further complicate matters for livestock producers, a wolf from Yellowstone National Park moved into the Upper Green in 1997 and began killing sheep before it was live-captured and moved back to the national park. It was the first confirmed wolf-killed livestock in the Upper Green for decades, but wolf presence would be documented in the area every year thereafter.

By the time the first of the cattle arrived in the Upper Green for the summer 1999 grazing season, the FWS issued a biological opinion declaring that continued livestock grazing was unlikely to jeopardize the recovery of grizzly bears.[25] The document included an incidental take statement limiting to four the number of bears that could be legally killed as nuisance animals before federal officials would have to be re-consulted. The document acknowledged the Upper Green is located outside the official grizzly bear recovery zone, thus bears occurring in the area were not necessary for the recovery of the species. And mortalities of grizzlies in the Upper Green were not to

After capturing a grizzly bear, WG&F's Zach Gregory examines the paw of an adult male grizzly bear that had repeatedly killed cattle in the Upper Green.

be considered when determining whether recovery goals were being met.

"The loss of individual bears could represent a negative impact to the grizzly bear population," the document stated. "However, this impact to the population should not hinder the eventual recovery of the species, because these bears are located more than ten miles outside of the recovery zone." According to FWS, the Upper Green was "not considered necessary for the survival and recovery of this species."

FWS also approved management guidelines for handling nuisance grizzlies in the Upper Green. With increased numbers of

Return of the Grizzly

Domestic sheep owned by the Thoman family graze in the Upper Green.

grizzlies killing both cattle and sheep in the region, FWS noted: "Recent attempts to manage these situations have been less than satisfactory. On the Bridger-Teton National Forest, bears had become trap shy or they leave the sheep herds for short periods, only to return and cause additional losses. As a result, grizzly bears are chronically preying on domestic sheep herds and are routinely killing cattle on these allotments. In some instances, adult females are likely conditioning young to use domestic sheep as a food source."

WG&F had spent more than one thousand man-hours responding to grizzly bear depredations on the Thoman sheep flocks during the prior grazing season. Sheep depredations had begun in 1996, with 113 sheep confirmed as grizzly kills, in addition to the forty-four cattle killed in a two-year period.

The new protocol required animal damage officials to spend six days from the start of losses in attempt to live capture and relocate any bear involved in sheep depredations, but if depredations continued beyond that point, authorization for lethal control could be granted. For cattle, lethal authorization would only be granted if losses due to the same bear continued for more than thirty days, or if depredations continued after five verified bear-killed cattle were documented in the same grazing season. All lethal control was contingent upon field personnel properly identifying the depredating bear. Because of the man-hours and technical skills needed, WG&F began contracting with USDA Wildlife Services to handle depredation problems in the Upper Green. WG&F, legally required to provide compensation to livestock losses due to trophy game animals, including the still federally protected grizzly bear, had already spent more than $67,000 compensating Upper Green livestock producers for verified losses to grizzly bears.

Shortly after adoption of the protocol, an adult male grizzly bear went on a killing spree in the Crow Creek area of the Upper Green's Pinyon Ridge, killing six cattle in four days.[26] It was a hot July day when Wildlife Services District Supervisor Merrill Nelson rode in on horseback to confirm the first two calf kills, then proceeded on to confirm a yearling beef had been killed as well. Nelson cut up the remains of the yearling carcass into three sections, dragging each parcel off to set leg snares for the bear. While he was setting the snares, Nelson looked up to see a huge male grizzly returning to claim the carcass, coming at him up the drag trail left from moving the carcass.

"I threw everything together into a bag, stepped into the saddle, and he loped towards me," Nelson said. "I just kept on going."

WG&F Trophy Game Coordinator Dave Moody pointed out, "Luckily he was on a horse."

It took several more nights of trapping before Nelson had Bear 269 in a leg snare. The bear weighed nearly 550 pounds, with a thirty-three-inch neck and was very scarred, with recent bites to his face and neck from encounters with other bears. Bear 269 had been the one bear officials had attempted to catch the year prior but the bear had evaded capture.

"It's the same area, the same time, the same track size, everything," Moody said. What was different was that he was killing at a much faster rate than in the past.

Bear 269 had a history. First trapped

A federal animal damage control official sets a snare.

Return of the Grizzly

and given a radio collar in the Dunoir area near Dubois three years earlier, Bear 269 moved into the Upper Green later the same year. Eventually he dropped his radio collar, and the by now trap-wary bear had been difficult to catch at previous kill sites. The bear was sedated and transferred to a culvert trap, which was then transported to Lander, where the bear was euthanized. State officials noted, "Chronic losses on this allotment in the past prompted the decision to remove #269 from the population."[27]

Four days later, the livestock killings began again; two more calves were mauled to death, and then five more were killed before the cattle left the allotment in the fall. Efforts to capture the offending bear were not successful.

Meanwhile, eight conservation groups sent a letter to FWS, asking the agency to revoke the new protocol, and for WG&F to cancel its contract with Wildlife Services for controlling damages.[28] The groups claimed that using Wildlife Services would result in the deaths of more grizzlies because of the agency's "clear history of and bias in favor of killing predators to protect livestock, rather than promoting the recovery of imperiled predators like the grizzly bear." The letter failed to acknowledge that Wildlife Services would be permitted to kill bears only with FWS authorization. The groups also attacked the livestock permittees, claiming that they were in violation of their grazing permits by not immediately removing livestock carcasses after bear kills. But removal of carcasses from remote mountain locations would be impossible, according to Bridger-Teton officials who noted that the livestock producers were doing a good job with carcass removal in areas where it was feasible. Ranchers were also dragging carcasses away from trails and recreational use areas.

Bridger-Teton District Ranger Bob Reese questioned the feasibility of finding dead sheep deep within a wilderness area, and if so, "What do you do with them?" The Thomans and Forest Service officials tried several different methods to destroy carcasses, and none were successful.

Several action groups signed the letter, including Biodiversity Associates, Greater Yellowstone Coalition, Jackson Hole Conservation Alliance, Predator Project, Sierra Club Grizzly Bear Ecosystems Project, Wyoming Chapter of Sierra Club, Wyoming Outdoor Council, and Wyoming Wildlife Federation.

After receiving the letter, WG&F Director John Baughman said conservation organizations needed to realize that the agencies were dealing with an expanding grizzly population, and as that population expands, conflicts will occur which must be dealt with. Adding that the conservative protocol was developed by the agencies with the best interest of the bear in mind, Baughman pointed to the fact that the Upper Green was miles from the recovery zone, and indeed outside the ten-mile perimeter used to monitor the bear population.

The criticism of the contract with Wildlife Services shouldn't be of concern either, he noted. "They are experts in dealing with livestock conflicts, with conflict resolution, damage investigation, and with catching bears," he said. Wildlife Services are well-trained professionals, Baughman noted. An added bonus is that Wildlife Services was authorized to respond to damage situations involving wolves, while WG&F personnel were not. So if a wolf killed cattle on the Upper Green, WG&F could respond, but if evidence indicated a wolf was involved, they would have to leave and call in Wildlife Services anyway.

WG&F assistant wildlife division chief (and eventually, director of the agency) Terry Cleveland was blunt, stating, "The reason we've got grizzly bears in the numbers and distribution we've got now is due to the personnel of the Wyoming Game and Fish Department—not the Fish and Wildlife Service, and not the land management agencies. We've been the ones on the ground, resolving conflicts."

Cleveland also pointed out that regardless of the protocol, Bear 269 was lethally removed after FWS authorized the action. "This bear was removed when and only when FWS authorized the action," he said. "We're not acting unilaterally. Wildlife Services is not acting unilaterally."

That September, livestock losses moved to the Leeds Creek area of the forest, about ten miles north of the Big Bend of the Green River.[29] Nelson found evidence that a three-hundred-pound sow grizzly and her two two-hundred-pound yearling cubs had killed five calves in one week. When he rode in on horseback to confirm the kills, he saw the three grizzlies feeding on a freshly killed calf.

"That grizzly was just tossing that calf—a five-hundred-pound bull calf—around like a rag doll," Nelson said. He set culvert traps and eventually captured all three grizzlies, after fourteen confirmed livestock kills on the allotment. The bears were moved to the Sunlight Basin area east of Yellowstone National Park.

Before capturing the bears, Nelson was able to watch them from a distance, as the sow circled a group of cattle.

"I am spellbound by the beauty and the power and the aggressiveness of a grizzly bear," Nelson said. "It's just unbelievable."

Relocation of problem bears was becoming an increasing problem for bear managers.

A state trap used to capture livestock-killing grizzly bears in the Upper Green.

Yellowstone National Park was saturated with bears, and would only accept bears if they were relocated into the backcountry via helicopter.[30] Park spokeswoman Cheryl Matthews noted: "We're just one-third of the grizzly bear recovery area. There are other areas where it would be appropriate to relocate bears. There are another two-thirds out there that is also appropriate bear habitat."

But Bridger-Teton officials felt that their agency's workload was already overburdened by grizzlies. Jackson District Ranger Nancy Hall said, "I don't really know that we're willing to take any more bears." With the expanding bear population,

Return of the Grizzly

areas suitable to relocate problem bears were limited.

Grizzly bear depredations on livestock had increased from eight confirmed cases in the early 1990s to more than seventy per year by the late 1990s. Most conflicts involving grizzlies occurred outside the official recovery zone—including conflicts with livestock, or property damage, as well as human-grizzly conflicts.

The Interagency Grizzly Bear Committee reported, "At present, highly selective control of livestock-depredating grizzly bears has resulted in only the most chronic depredators being removed from the Yellowstone population. Depredation on livestock will likely continue to increase as grizzly bear activity outside of the designated Recovery Zone increases. At some point the level of human tolerance of grizzly bear depredations on livestock will likely be exceeded,

especially in areas far from the Recovery Zone boundary. At that point, predator control actions against depredating grizzly bears will likely increase as well."[31]

Conservation organizations remained focused on not just maintaining the existing grizzly bear population, but strived for increased protections across a much broader historic range. It seemed that every proposal that was brought forth in the Yellowstone region was subject to criticism or litigation, and the chasm with bear managers grew wider even as the grizzly population grew.

FWS grizzly bear recovery coordinator Chris Servheen wrote in the journal *Ursus*:

Reliance on regulatory authority and litigation to restrict public access and resource extraction on public lands usually leads to polarization and builds

The grizzly bear—long gone from the Upper Green—had returned.

local resentment against bears. The solution to building public support is to focus on local communities and their interests and to address the threats they perceive about bears. In most cases local people believe that threats are not coming from the bears themselves, but from the lawyers, litigants, and others who use the grizzly to achieve results on other issues such as road access or timber harvest. This litigious approach eliminates involvement of local communities and promotes antagonism rather than cooperation.[32]

By the late 1990s, most conflicts involving grizzlies occurred outside the bear recovery zone.

Return of the Grizzly

CHAPTER 4

SEASONAL FOOD AVAILABILITY

Carrion from ungulates that died during winter is an important food source from grizzlies emerging from their winter dens.

Grizzlies will eat just about anything. They graze on grass, overturn rocks for insects, dig for roots, tubers, and earthworms, strip berries from bushes, run down large mammals, slap grouse from the air, rip open logs to lick up ants, tear branches from trees to access apples, churn up earth for pocket gophers and voles, snatch fish from streams, and steal pine nut seeds cached by hard-working squirrels preparing for winter. This food-opportunist behavior serves them well as they move across their range, shifting their diets to take advantage of the seasonal foods available.

Conservationists worried that with changes in food composition in the Yellowstone region after the closure of the park's dumps, what had been the change in the diet of the region's grizzlies? Changes in the region's bear foods would become a point of contention for decades to come.

When Yellowstone's grizzlies emerge from their winter dens in spring, they key on carrion from winter-killed ungulates such as elk and bison. But the abundance of carrion at this time is influenced by the severity of the previous winter, and after gray wolves were reintroduced into Yellowstone Park in 1995 and 1996, competition for available carrion increased with increasing wolf numbers.

Grizzlies tend to switch from carrion to preying on elk calves during the calving season in May and June. Grizzly bear bones discovered in a thousand-year-old packrat midden (a food storage area characterized by accumulated debris) in Yellowstone National Park's Lamar Cave indicate the bear's historic diet consisted of 32 percent meat, and 68 percent plants—the same ratio found in grizzly bears killed in the nineteenth century in Montana and Wyoming. Today, adult female and subadult grizzlies in Yellowstone consume about 40 percent meat, and 60 percent plants. Adult males, who are more capable of taking down large animals and can dominate carcasses, have high meat consumption, at 80 percent, with only 20 percent plant matter. Bears outside the park that prey on livestock have even higher meat consumption: 85 percent (which is the same ratio of meat:plant consumption as the bears that fed on garbage in Yellowstone in the early 1900s).[33]

These statistics are very different from other grizzly bear populations, with Glacier and Denali National Park bears consuming only 3 percent meat to 97 percent plants, or Alaska's salmon-fed grizzlies with their 72 percent meat to 28 percent plant diet.

Grizzly bear researchers in Yellowstone National Park have taken notice of the strategies grizzly bears use in their hunting for meat. Husband-wife research team Steve and Marilyn French documented three major hunting strategies used by grizzlies in pursuit of elk.[34] The first method is the search for elk calves, in which bears hunt in a zigzag pattern through patches of sagebrush with noses to the ground. This strategy proved successful even when there

were no adult elk in sight to suggest calves would be present.

The second method involves a chase. A bear charges at a group of cow and calf elk, trying to separate an individual calf from the herd and run it down. Calves that ran in a straight line could get away, but grizzlies succeeded in killing calves that ran in an arc by "heading 'em off at the pass." Incidentally, a study conducted by Francis Singer, Kate Symonds, and Bill Berger in the park from 1988 to 1992 showed that grizzlies were one of the most significant predators of elk calves, killing about 950 calves on the northern range of the park each year. Grizzlies killed as many calves as black bears and coyotes combined.

The third elk hunting method used by grizzlies is the ambush, in which a grizzly charges out of the timber at herds of elk in open meadows or sagebrush. Researchers Kerry Gunther and R. Renkin found Yel-

Grizzlies switch their food preferences to elk calves during the May and June elk birthing season.

Return of the Grizzly

lowstone grizzlies chased elk an average of 8.7 minutes in each attack. Forty-five percent of the chases observed by researchers resulted in capture of at least one elk calf.[35]

The number of ungulates available to grizzly bears in Yellowstone shrank with the park's elk population after wolves were reintroduced. The northern range elk herd was estimated at seventeen thousand animals in 1995, the year wolves were placed in the park. By 2013, the elk herd had dropped to less than four thousand animals. Bear researchers noted, "Competition for the ungulate resource likely has increased due to an approximate three-fold increase in grizzly numbers since the 1970s and growth of the reintroduced wolf population from thirty-one individuals in 1995 to a minimum of 463 in the Greater Yellowstone Ecosystem in 2012."[36]

Grizzly bear breeding season is from about mid-May through mid-July, and in addition to elk calves, many of the park's grizzlies traditionally concentrate on spawning cutthroat trout, a summer food source rich in protein. The discovery of non-native lake trout in Yellowstone Lake in 1994 raised red flags of alarm with park managers. The unchecked invasion of lake trout was predicted to cause a decline of up to 90 percent of cutthroats as the lake invader ate the smaller, native trout population. "The lake trout discovery in Yellowstone Lake has the potential to cause a precipitous decline in the cutthroat trout population and bear use of cutthroat trout."[37] By 2000, spawning cutthroats had undergone substantial reductions, and more than twelve thousand lake trout were netted by researchers trying to rid park waters of the species.

Late summer is characterized by the onset of early hyperphagia, the season in which grizzlies engage in intensive search for high-energy foods needed to pack on fat reserves to survive winter hibernation. During this time, many Yellowstone region grizzlies key

Grizzlies raid food middens containing nuts cached by American red squirrels.

Seasonal Food Availability

on army cutwork moths, and whitebark pine nuts—two important food sources that are subject to natural fluctuations.

The Interagency Grizzly Bear Study Team reported that grizzlies consume whitebark pine seeds to the near exclusion of other foods when the seeds are available in adequate quantities—as they were in 1996, when trees averaged twenty-five cones per tree, the highest recording since 1989. Whitebark pine seeds are an important, high-fat content food that bears key in on in fall. Bear managers noted that in years of low whitebark pine seed availability, grizzlies wander further as they seek alternative food sources, which often leads to conflicts with human activities and results in management actions or mortalities of bears, especially during the fall months. The period 1993 through 1995 was one of low whitebark pine seed production, and bear managers had corresponding increases in the numbers of management captures of grizzlies involved in conflicts. Park officials reported overall poor food conditions for grizzlies throughout much of 1994, with 124 resulting reports of property damage and nine grizzly-caused human injuries.[38] While bear-inflicted human injuries used to occur along park roadsides and often involved black bears, that changed from 1980 to 1994, when most injuries occurred in the backcountry, and 84 percent of those injuries were caused by grizzlies, and tended to be more severe.[39]

Grizzly bear use of army cutworm moth (ACM) sites high on talus slopes was first documented in Montana's Mission Mountains in 1952, but it wasn't until the mid-1980s that researchers discovered that ACM serve as a key food source for grizzlies in the Yellowstone region. There were eight known moth sites in the Yellowstone region in 1986, which increased to forty-three sites by 1998 as researchers sought to document grizzly bear use of these sites. Bear managers documented 44 percent of all known grizzlies in the Yellowstone ecosystem using the sites located in the Absaroka Mountains of Wyoming in the early 1990s, and that female grizzlies comprised 40 percent of these bears.

In 1996, an adult female grizzly, Bear 284, was relocated by state officials after being trapped following a domestic sheep depredation.[40] Originally located in the western portion of Grand Teton National Park, she was transported to the North Fork of the Shoshone River (located east of Yellowstone Park) and released wearing a tracking collar. It's not known if she discovered any ACM sites that fall, but bear managers suspect she must have. The sow grizzly denned in the North Fork area, but upon emerging from her den the next spring, she moved back across the ecosystem to the area from which she had originally been captured. The collar allowed researchers to track her movements in the fall of 1998 as she traveled with her cubs from the southwestern portion of the ecosystem back to the Shoshone River country. Not only did Bear 284 show a dramatically larger home range than most other grizzlies in the ecosystem, but this cross-ecosystem movement was significant in another way. She had moved from a part of the ecosystem without insect aggregation sites to an area where the insects were available. In taking her cubs on her migration, she was passing down this food knowledge to the next generation. Greg Holm of the Wyoming Game and Fish Department noted the importance of this "cultural inheritance of knowledge regarding insect aggregation sites spreading from one portion of the ecosystem to another."

Biologists believed that as grizzlies move to high elevations to forage on ACM and whitebark pine nuts in the fall, in the process they take themselves away from roads and areas of human activity, thus conflicts are reduced. However, if the ACM or whitebark pine nuts are absent or reduced in some years, conflicts increase as grizzlies range further and in lower elevations seeking food during late hyperphagia. As with other important food sources, years with poor moth populations have substantially more nuisance bear management activities.

While bear managers pointed to the grizzly bear's habit of switching to various foods that become seasonally available within its habitat, conservation groups argued that the overall decline in several important food sources in the region was a critical loss for grizzlies that would result in more bear deaths as bears sought out foods in closer proximity to people—including their increased reliance on meat in the form of livestock.

Whitebark pine cone and seeds. US Geological Survey photo by Suzanna Soileau.

Seasonal Food Availability

CHAPTER 5

FRUSTRATIONS MOUNT

A grizzly sow and her young cub along a river in western Wyoming.

By 1998, bear managers were frustrated with the continued fight with conservationists over grizzly bears. WG&F Director John Baughman penned an editorial in *Wyoming Wildlife News* calling for grizzlies to be removed from the list of protected species, noting, "We now find ourselves trying to work a grizzly bear recovery plan through a legal/political/technical morass that, by its very nature, ensures that a recovery plan would be outdated before it could ever be implemented."[41]

He wrote, "We are still arguing over recovery criteria for bear numbers, geographic distribution, acceptable human-caused mortality and habitat requirements, when the time is already upon us to decide where we really want grizzlies and how to deal with problem bears in different areas."

Baughman said while the number of grizzlies in the state was the subject of much debate, "what is certain is that more bears are getting into trouble over a broader area than ever before." Baughman contended that delisting needed to occur because the bear was losing local support due to the costs and problems associated with "an expanding bear population and frustrations over a lack of progress made toward delisting." Grizzlies would be better served by delisting, Baughman wrote, and "Secondly, I contend we already have more bears in more places that the public or the US Fish and Wildlife Service could or would tolerate if it wasn't for WG&F's programs of conflict resolution, damage prevention, damage payment and public education." The state's portion for management of this federally protected species was already creeping up toward $1 million annually.

Residents far outside the recovery zone had already altered their behaviors in response to grizzly bear presence. The first reports of grizzlies emerging from their dens (in recent years, as early as February) serves as a sign to wildlife lovers throughout the ecosystem to take down their bird feeders lest they attract bears. With assistance from WG&F, rural beekeepers throughout western Wyoming erected electric fences to keep their hives safe.

Families who journeyed to their favorite lake each summer found the presence of grizzly bears in the willows alongshore too high a risk for their family excursions in Sublette County.

After numerous livestock depredations by grizzlies moving in to new areas, sheep and cattle producers in Idaho and Wyoming agreed to buyouts that allowed federal agencies to close their former allotments to livestock grazing.

Foodies seeking to harvest natural berries gave up the practice when they learned bears inhabited the same briar patches in southwestern Montana, seeking out those same berries.

A grizzly bear tests a bear-proof garbage can.

Game bird hunters were no longer willing to approach patches of brush from which birds can be flushed, never knowing if it they will be met with a covey of birds or a charging grizzly.

Small rural apple orchards or trees planted years ago by previous generations become bear attractants as well. Residents who enjoyed watching deer and other wildlife come to their Park County homesteads to nibble on apples that fell from the trees were cautioned to chop down the trees to reduce the attractant. Those who resisted getting rid of their trees began the daily routine of picking up fallen apples so the bears wouldn't find any when they inevitably arrived.

Throughout the tri-state area, residents had learned to keep their garbage and livestock feed in areas inaccessible to bears. Their pets could no longer be fed outside or on porches. Carcass dumps on ranches and rural landfills were buried or discontinued. Backpackers with small children avoided mountain hikes in the Blackrock area south of Moran, Wyoming, fearing the squealing/ sounds of a small child strapped to their back could initiate an attack.

Hikers who had trekked the same trails year after year from the time they were in scouts, refused to traverse well-loved routes in the Wind Rivers.

How many more bears, and how much more change, was going to be expected of area residents?

It was a fairly quiet grazing season for the cattle in the Upper Green, with a half-dozen confirmed grizzly kills, but grizzlies were hitting the Thoman sheep flocks hard, with more than forty confirmed kills, and sheep scattering in all directions due to the attacks.[42] WG&F suspected one adult grizzly

Thoman sheep going to water in the Upper Green.

Return of the Grizzly

was responsible for most of the sheep deaths, and noted that the continued sheep depredations only counted as one strike against the bear. Only if the bear was relocated from the area and then preyed on livestock again would it have a second strike against it and become a candidate for permanent removal from the population. That a bear could kill so many livestock and still have only one mark against it was a demonstration of how preposterous the situation had become for area livestock producers. Inflexible federal rules that protected problem grizzlies added to the increased distain for keeping the bears under federal management.

In one late July incident, the bear attacked and scattered the sheep in one of the Thoman flocks. It was two days before the hundred-odd missing sheep were discovered making their way out of the timber in small groups. Herders spent four or five days searching for and gathering what sheep they could find. There were no confirmed kills in the incident, but once all the sheep were gathered back together, the bear came back to attack the herd again. Mary Thoman said it was as if the bear's food source in the timber had been taken away and the bear returned to retrieve it. The Thomans wouldn't know until they counted their sheep off the forest at the end of the season exactly how many were missing.

Later in August, after going out to try to find and gather missing sheep from the last attack on his flock, one of the Thoman sheepherders failed to return to camp that night.[43] He arrived back the next morning, and reported being charged and run up a tree by two grizzlies (a sow with a yearling) while on his way back to camp with the sheep the previous evening. As he clung to the tree, the sow swiped him on the leg, tearing his pant leg, and the yearling bear

Mary Thoman checks in with one of the herders tending to the family's sheep.

tried to bite the toe of the boot on his other foot, but the herder sprayed the bears in the face with pepper spray. All of the Thoman Ranch employees carry canisters of pepper spray on their belts while the sheep graze in the Upper Green.

The herder, who does not speak fluent English, was unharmed, but investigators were not able to confirm his story, and publicly cast doubt as to whether the incident actually occurred. Regardless, the herder had returned to his flock after an overnight outing, and returned with an empty canister of bear spray.

An incident a month later would add

weight to the herder's report of a sow and her yearling in the area.[44] Two bowhunters, a father and son team, were walking through a meadow in the Upper Green when they were charged by a sow grizzly with a yearling cub. According to the game warden that interviewed the pair, the yearling knocked the father down. When the son yelled at the bear and began to approach his father on the ground, the bear charged the son. The son either was knocked down or fell down, and the son put his legs into the air.

"It catapulted the bear right over the top of him," the warden said. The bears fled the scene and neither hunter was injured.

That October, an elk hunter was mauled by a grizzly sow accompanied by three yearlings just off the Flagstaff Road near Togwotee Pass. The man's hunting partner then shot and killed the sow. The injured hunter was evacuated via helicopter and taken to an Idaho hospital for treatment. No attempts were made to capture the yearling bears.

Wyoming lawmakers had grown weary of waiting for grizzlies to be delisted while Wyoming was footing much of the bill toward bear management and recovery.[45] A state senator proposed legislation that would retract WG&F's responsibility to pay for livestock losses caused by grizzly bears. The lawmaker said his primary reason for advancing the proposal was because of the unfairness that grizzly recovery was a federally mandated program but required Wyoming to foot the bill. After Upper Green rancher Charles Price explained to a legislative committee that the proposal would shift the total burden of livestock losses onto producers, the senator withdrew his proposal.

The summer of 1999 would eventually be known as the season of the tent-hopping

A tent that was jumped on by a grizzly bear (nicknamed Kelty) in Yellowstone National Park's Indian Creek campground. National Park Service photo by Jim Peaco, July 1999.

Return of the Grizzly

grizzly in Yellowstone National Park. It began one early morning in late June, when a subadult grizzly bear entered a campsite in the Indian Creek Campground and pawed a tent, ripping the tent pole sleeve and breaking the pole, but not causing human injury. Ten days later, the bear returned to the campground, sticking his head into the screen door of an occupied tent, only to retreat when yelled at by the tent's occupants. He ambled over to lean on the next tent, breaking its aluminum pole as the tent's occupants yelled at him to scramble. The bear continued on its journey, digging for food scraps in the ashes of fire pits in the campground before it stepped on another occupied tent, bending the tent poles and tearing the rain fly, but again retreating. No one was injured in any of the incidents, and the National Park Service set traps to try to capture the marauding bear. A young female bear was captured and relocated away from the area, but while she was known to be away, the tent vandalism continued.

In mid-July, two subadult bears entered the Indian Creek Campground despite the efforts of campers who banged pots, yelled at the bears, and honked their car horns. One bear held back, but another walked up to a tent and "bounced" on its side, breaking the tent poles, ripping its fabric, and crushing it to the ground. When trapping efforts failed to capture the badly behaved bruin, park officials prohibited the use of soft-sided tents in the campground and problems at the campground ended.

It took a few weeks, but the problem migrated to another location about seven miles away from the campground. In mid-August, the bear was at it again, jumping on a tent, breaking its poles and tearing holes in the fabric, as its former occupant watched

A young male grizzly bear.

from the safety of a nearby tree. Another group of campers reported a similar event earlier the same night, so park officials shut down all backcountry campsites in the area. On August 22, 1999, a subadult male grizzly bear was finally captured in a trap near the Indian Creek Campground when a decoy tent was set near a trap. He fell for the bait and was captured. By this time, the bear had deposited his DNA on six damaged tents.

Agency officials debated what to do with the bear, but finally determined that the animal was a danger to public safety as outlined in federal rules, which called for the bear's removal from the population. The bear was held at the Grizzly Discovery Center in West Yellowstone, Montana, while attempts were made to find it a new home. The bear was eventually moved to a private non-profit animal sanctuary in California. The short reign of the tent-crushing Yellowstone grizzly had ended.

A sign warning the public that there is no guarantee of safety in bear country.

Return of the Grizzly

CHAPTER 6

HUNTING ATTRACTANTS

A large boar grizzly scratches his back on a utility pole.

With so many grizzlies ranging far outside the recovery zone, conflicts between big game hunters and grizzly bears went from being rare occasions to a regular occurrence in the late 1990s. By 1999, according to WG&F, "Losing meat left in the field to bear scavenging has become a common and expected occurrence in northwestern Wyoming."[46]

Yellowstone's pioneering bear researchers, the Craighead brothers, had coined the term ecocenter to describe "a site with a large, dependable source of high-calorie food that seasonally attracts and holds large aggregations of bears for periods of two to three months."[47] The ecocenter concept rang true for grizzly bears as they turned from the park's dumps to ungulate carcasses downed by hunters, and later, caraway plants in southwestern Montana, and cattle in the Upper Green of western Wyoming.

Mark Haroldson and other members of the Interagency Grizzly Bear Study Team found that when the elk hunting season opened in mid-September in southern Montana, marked Yellowstone National Park grizzly bears abruptly left the park's northern boundary and headed to the ungulate remains left by hunters. "This shift creates a situation in which large numbers of grizzly bears are in close association with large numbers of armed humans during a season when bears are driven to forage."

They noted, "Ungulate harvest and wounding loss by hunters may influence the fall distribution of grizzly bears by creating dispersed 'ecocenters'" much in the same way that grizzlies congregate on trout streams, insect aggregation sites, garbage dumps, or other important seasonal food sources. "Bears learn to use available food resources quickly, and when food availability becomes predictable, bears establish traditional use and impart that behavior to their offspring."[48]

In addition, "Approximately two bear generations have passed since legal hunting stopped and grizzly bears in the Greater Yellowstone Ecosystem were given protected status. During this time, the long-standing tradition of early elk harvest seasons adjacent to Yellowstone National Park has provided considerable food resources to bears, with presumably little negative impact (for bears not killed in conflicts) from increasing familiarization with humans. Because bears learn quickly and females pass on learned behaviors to their offspring, two generations seems ample time and the motivation exists for a pattern of traditional use to be expressed."

Other researchers in the mid-1980s had looked at the food resources left behind by elk hunters in the Yellowstone ecosystem as they harvested or wounded elk in legal elk hunts, with an annual estimate of 370 tons

A radio-collared grizzly in Grand Teton National Park.

Return of the Grizzly

of biomass left by hunters in the form of gut piles and other discarded parts.

Hunters had long suggested that grizzly bears respond to a rifle shot like a ranch crew coming to a dinner bell, with bears approaching hunter-killed elk in anticipation of the gut pile feast left remaining in the field. Researchers in Grand Teton National Park tracked movements of GPS-collared grizzlies, finding in the first field season that at least one grizzly bear followed elk hunters seeking out their game—without the hunters being aware that the grizzly was following their movements. The hunters had volunteered to carry GPS units during their day hunt for elk in Grand Teton's annual elk reduction program. At one point the grizzly was within one hundred yards of the hunters, yet the hunters never realized there was a bear nearby.[49]

During the 1990s, the largest source of grizzly bear mortality in the Yellowstone region was hunting-related, as more human hunters encountered more grizzlies across an expanded range. In the fall of 1992, a bighorn sheep hunter surprised a sow grizzly with cubs as they slept in their daybeds in Sunlight Basin east of the park.[50] When the sow stood up and saw the man, she charged, knocking him to the ground and mauling him. As he was being mauled, the hunter managed to chamber a round in his rifle and fired a shot into the air, causing the bear to flee. The hunter then walked to his horse, rode it down the trail to his vehicle, and drove himself to the nearest hospital. The man had extensive injuries requiring several hundred stiches, but no broken bones.

Prior to 1999, records of human-grizzly bear conflicts in the Yellowstone region were kept by a variety of agencies without

A sow grizzly with two yearlings.

a central repository to compile the information from various sources. In 1999, the Yellowstone Ecosystem Subcommittee of the Interagency Grizzly Bear Committee assigned this task to Yellowstone National Park. Grizzlies caused only two human injuries that year, and both incidents occurred within Yellowstone Park.[51] In the first incident, a couple had a surprise encounter with a sow grizzly and her two yearlings. The sow swatted the man on the leg as the couple "played dead" on the ground and the man deployed pepper spray. About a month later, a man hiking alone on the same trail had a similar encounter with a sow and two yearlings. When the sow charged, the man attempted to play dead but as the attack progressed he began to fight back. He survived the mauling.

In 2000, FWS amended the Grizzly Bear Recovery Plan to clarify that only known human-caused grizzly bear mortalities occurring within the Yellowstone Grizzly Bear Recovery Zone and a ten-mile perimeter area count against mortality quotas. In addition, beginning in 2000, probable mortalities were included in the calculation of mortality thresholds, and cubs orphaned as a result of human causes would also be designated as probable mortalities.[52]

The year proved to be another dry one, with extended drought and wildfires flaring through Wyoming, and a high number of hunter-related grizzly bear mortalities. Of the twenty-three known grizzly bear mortalities in the ecosystem, sixteen were hunting related, including several cases of black bear hunters mistakenly killing grizzlies, grizzlies killed after entering elk hunting camps, and grizzlies killed while the bears were attempting to claim hunter-killed elk carcasses, as well as chance encounters by hunters. In one case, a grizzly bear grabbed a deer that was being dragged out by a hunter and was shot and killed in the encounter. At least one human received injuries from a grizzly in one of these hunter encounters.

Soon after the coordinated recordkeeping of human-grizzly conflicts began, hunting's role in the conflicts became apparent. The IGBST reported, "The annual number of hunting-related grizzly bear mortalities has been increasing since the early 1990s and suggests an upward trend. Factors likely contributing to this trend were an increasing and expanding grizzly bear population and possibly a seasonal increase in bear densities in early elk harvest area."[53]

"The need for grizzly bear management efforts will become ever-demanding in the future," bear managers wrote in 2000. "We can no longer assume that areas outside of the Recovery Zone are not occupied by grizzly bears. During 1998, a grizzly bear killed livestock eighty miles from the Recovery Zone boundary."[54]

A shepherd tending to a band of sheep in the Pat O'Hara region of the Shoshone National Forest northwest of Cody shot, killed, and buried an adult male grizzly bear after the bear attacked his flock, killing three sheep. The carcass was discovered, and both the sheepherder and the flock owner were fined in the incident.

There were more than 150 grizzly-human conflicts in 2000—everything from bears obtaining (or attempting to gain) non-natural foods (human, livestock, or pet food, garbage, etc.), to damaging private property, killing livestock, and injuring humans. Nearly 60 percent of these incidents occurred on private property (most in Wyoming) and occurred outside the grizzly bear recovery zone.[55]

There were ninety-seven cases of grizzly bear–human confrontations, including four

Many conflicts occur when grizzlies approach areas of human development.

cases of human injuries due to grizzlies in the Yellowstone region that year. In two cases, grizzlies claimed and would not give up hunter-killed ungulate carcasses. In forty-eight cases, grizzlies entered developed areas, and twenty-two cases of aggressive interactions involving no human injuries, twelve cases involving grizzlies approaching or following people, and eleven incidents where grizzlies entered occupied backcountry camps.

Grizzly bear depredations on livestock had increased significantly outside the recovery zone, and on private land, from 1992 to 2000, rising from eight incidents in 1992 to a high of seventy-three incidents in 1997, and remaining high thereafter. In such cases, there often was more than one livestock death per incident. Bear managers noted that grizzlies appeared to kill sheep

and cattle regardless of the abundance of natural bear foods.[56]

Grizzly bear conflicts were consistent in the Upper Green River region north of Pinedale (where grizzlies had routinely preyed on cattle and sheep since the mid-1990s) and in the North and South Forks of the Shoshone River area near Cody (where bears killed cattle and sheep; damaged apiaries, orchards, buildings, and vehicles; and obtained garbage). Bear managers focused on removing specific, chronic livestock-killing bears, noting that it was "the most effective method of alleviating livestock losses while having minimal impact on the long-term survival of the grizzly bear population."[57]

In 2000, it was reported that there were seventy-four known human-caused grizzly bear mortalities during the previous nine

Hunting Attractants

A sow grizzly sleeps in a meadow.

years, and 43 percent were cases involving killing a bear in defense of life and property, while management removals constituted another 31 percent. Other sources of mortality included: poaching, 12 percent; mistaken identity by black bear hunters, 7 percent; electrocution by downed power lines, 4 percent; and bears killed by vehicles, 3 percent.

The greatest source of human-caused grizzly bear mortality in the Yellowstone ecosystem had become self-defense killing, accounting for 43 percent of human-caused mortalities from 1992 to 2000.[58]

Preceded by two dry summers, 2001 offered little change, and escalating conflicts between humans and grizzlies throughout the Yellowstone ecosystem soon followed. In 2001, there were more than two hundred grizzly bear–human conflicts reported in

the Yellowstone ecosystem, with substantial increases in conflicts reported in areas outside the grizzly bear recovery zone as the grizzly population continued to expand. Grand Teton National Park had an unprecedented four human-grizzly conflicts, including three involving human injuries.[59]

According to Park Service officials, in early March 2001, a Park Service employee was attacked by a grizzly while cross-country skiing at 9:30 p.m. by the light of a nearly full moon—an incident reported as "perhaps the first such recorded confrontation in North America." The bear walked more than three hundred yards across an open meadow to deliberately approach the skier, then charged from a distance of twenty yards. The skier dropped to the ground and was involved in a short scuffle in which the bear bit the skier's arm and

Return of the Grizzly

thigh before the bear walked away in the direction from which it had come.

A month later, a fisherman was followed by a young male grizzly near the Snake River Bridge at Flagg Ranch. The fisherman worked his way up onto the bridge, where the bear attacked, biting the man's arm. The man began to fight back and a passing vehicle approached, at which point the bear fled the scene.

All was quiet until the fall, during the park's annual elk hunt. Shortly after spotting a small bear running away from him in the Moran area, a hunter was charged and hit from his right side by a sow grizzly. The man was mauled but survived, and the encounter was viewed as consistent with a sow bear with cubs exhibiting normal defensive behavior.

A week later and less than six hundred yards from the Snake River Bridge fisherman incident that happened earlier in the year, it appeared the young male grizzly was at it again. A park maintenance worker was repairing a sign in the riverside picnic area when he heard something behind him. He turned to find a grizzly bear standing just six feet away, looking at him. The man yelled for the bear to go away, and when the bear failed to move, the man began backing away. He made it safely to the confines of his nearby pickup truck, and afterwards, the bear departed.

Although the incident ended without injury, this subadult male grizzly had distinct white markings around its neck and on its chest that made its identification fairly simple. Throughout the year, the bear was reported to have approached numerous hikers, entered camps, and looked into the back of a pickup truck.

A sow with young cubs charged a bowhunter in the fall of 2001, but officials suspect the attack was normal defensive behavior.

Hunting Attractants

Confrontational conflicts between humans and grizzlies continued to increase in the Montana portion of the ecosystem as well, with grizzlies confirmed more than forty miles from the recovery zone. Montana officials reported that from 1992 to 2001, twelve people were injured in grizzly bear attacks. One archery hunter was injured in 2001 while elk hunting after a sow grizzly charged and attacked him (the sow was accompanied by two yearling cubs), and two grizzlies were killed in backcountry self-defense situations in 2000.

Other conflicts occurred in southern Montana, and while they did not involve human injury, they were startling. In July 2001, an adult male grizzly tried to break into a house in Cooke City while a person was inside. The bear was seen on numerous porches, and checking doors and windows of other houses. After attempts to haze the bear away from human developments failed, bear managers captured and killed the bear because of the danger it posed to humans.

An adult female grizzly was captured and placed into a zoo in 2001 because of its track record of seeking out unnatural foods and increasingly bold behavior. All told, the bear had been involved in fifty-five incidents in a three-year period.

Montana bear managers warned that "The need for grizzly bear management efforts will become ever-demanding in the future," as recovery efforts succeeded, and the population continued to expand its range.

Wyoming also saw huge increases in human-grizzly conflicts in 2001, with 188 incidents—a 215 percent increase from the previous five-year average of eighty-eight incidents each year. Although it was a dry summer and fall, with bears searching widely

A grizzly bear crosses a road in Yellowstone National Park.

Return of the Grizzly

for foods, the increasing bear population and its continued range expansion also accounted for the increase in conflicts. The reduction in cattle depredations by grizzlies in Wyoming that year was offset by the huge increase in depredations on sheep in the Upper Green River region, with bear managers trapping three subadult male bears from the area and translocating them elsewhere after repeated depredations. State officials killed thirteen grizzlies in Wyoming in 2001 after repeated conflicts with humans.

Yellowstone officials also recorded numerous cases of grizzlies approaching people at camps or in picnic areas, with the bears eating whatever human food that remained when the people backed away. In another case, a park ranger heard a noise at the door of his house and looked out to see a bear standing on its hind legs looking in the window. The bear ripped out the screen on the front door, and damaged the windowpanes on several windows near the door as it attempted to gain entry. The ranger yelled, and the bear eventually wandered away.

Grizzlies shifted movements to take advantage of hunter-killed ungulates.

CHAPTER 7

PUBLIC FRACAS

A boar grizzly bear in the Yellowstone ecosystem.

As the Interagency Grizzly Bear Committee (IGBC) and the US Fish and Wildlife Service (FWS) prepared to push forward with plans to eventually remove bears from federal protection, animal activists protested every move. To prepare for delisting, much work had to be done by the agencies within IGBC. All the agencies needed to get a handle on the number of hunter-killed grizzlies, and get more members of the public to start keeping clean camps, so an expanded food storage order would need to be brought forth to cover lands administered by the Shoshone and Bridger-Teton National Forests. Each of the three state wildlife management agencies needed to adopt plans detailing how states would manage bears once they were no longer under federal protection. At the federal level, FWS was required to craft a Conservation Strategy that would ensure adequate regulatory mechanisms were in place to protect the bear population and its habitat after delisting. The national forests would need to amend their forest plans to incorporate components of the habitat provisions of the Conservation Strategy. The public was flooded with proposed federal, state, and local policies that would probably have little or no impact to those living outside the region, but would have real impacts to residents of the Yellowstone ecosystem.

WG&F used a twenty-one-member citizen panel to craft its draft management plan in 2001. The plan would allow grizzly bear population dispersion throughout the Yellowstone ecosystem to areas that were "biologically suitable and socially acceptable." Emphasis on proper food storage would occur in areas of expansion, but outside of the grizzly bear recovery zone (which would be redesignated as the Primary Conservation Area, or "PCA") lower densities of bears would be expected, and agencies were to work to "achieve a balance between multiple use and the security needs of the grizzly bear, realizing that grizzly bears outside the PCA are not critical to the long-term survival of the bear in the Greater Yellowstone Ecosystem."[60] Nuisance bears would be managed under federal guidelines within the PCA, but outside the PCA, "when applicable, lethal take of nuisance grizzly bears by affected property owners will be allowed through special authorizations from WG&F." State bear managers had a range of alternatives for handling bears, from no action, to aversive conditioning, and deterrence and removal. The plan also laid the framework for eventual "take" of nuisance grizzlies deemed appropriate for removal, should the state develop regulations for such harvest.

In June 2001, state bear managers were bracing for escalating conflicts on national forest grazing allotments as cattle entered their mountain pastures under continued dry conditions. By mid-July, two subadult male grizzlies were relocated away from the Upper Green after killings involving both sheep and cattle, and within a few weeks, a third male grizzly was moved for the same reason. A fourth subadult male was captured and radio collared after he was reported to be visiting a bait set out by a black bear hunter in the Jim Creek area north of New Fork Lakes in the Upper Green. At that point, this research bear was the southernmost bear confirmed in Wyoming since recovery efforts had begun in the 1970s. But by early August, the Jim Creek bear was dead, killed by state wildlife officials after tearing up one backcountry camp and entering the town of Dubois three nights in a row. WG&F bear management officer Brian DeBolt said: "It was extremely dangerous. People made a potentially dangerous situation even more dangerous by approaching him so close" as they sought to take photos of the town grizzly.[61] State officials set a culvert trap in the residential yard to capture the bear before euthanizing him.

"He was a threat to human safety," DeBolt added. "He had to be destroyed before someone got hurt. There was no other alternative."

By mid-August, WG&F's Mark Bruscino said his agency was getting so many bear calls that the state wildlife agency was having a hard time keeping up. Dry conditions resulted in a lot of bear activity at lower elevations and along drainages.

Riders for the Upper Green Cattle Association reported seeing six different grizzlies in one day while checking cattle, but since the Upper Green is located outside the official bear recovery zone, these bears didn't count as part of the progress toward recovery.[62] Big Piney cattleman Eddie Wardell expressed concern for other users of the national forest being in such close contact with grizzlies, especially small children playing near their parent's camping locations in the Upper Green. Environmental groups were already threatening to sue should delisting move forward, which WG&F hoped would occur by 2004. Wildfires throughout the Bridger-Teton that summer kept fire crews busy, and the new acting Forest Service district ranger in Pinedale who took office (after his predecessor was forced out) promptly issued citations to various permitted users of the Upper Green, including the Thoman family, for allowing their domestic sheep to bed in the same area on too many occasions. On these occasions, the sheep were intentionally bedded in the same place while bear managers set traps in attempt to catch grizzlies that were repeatedly preying on the flock. But the wildlife damage specialists setting the traps were also in trouble, as the Forest Service sent a letter of reprimand to USDA Wildlife Services for driving an ATV along a streamside and on closed road—both instances while setting bear traps. Neither letter was well received by its recipients who had been knee-deep in bear problems all grazing season, and the acting district ranger only managed to serve in that position for less than three months before moving on.[63] All involved appeared relieved with the arrival of fall snows as the livestock left their grazing allotments, the wildfires were out, and bears entered their winter dens.

The 2001–02 winter had relatively mild conditions, so there were fewer winter-killed ungulate carcasses for grizzlies emerging from their dens to scavenge on, and as the summer progressed it became evident that not only were spawning cutthroat

A grizzly bear crosses a road in Yellowstone National Park as traffic stops.

Return of the Grizzly

trout numbers low, but whitebark pine cone production was poor throughout the ecosystem as well. As expected, human-grizzly conflicts escalated, with a record high of 249 incidents reported throughout the ecosystem, with more than half the conflicts occurring outside the bear recovery zone.[64] Both cattle and sheep depredations in Wyoming increased, and bear managers relocated or killed six grizzlies in response to continued conflicts involving these bears.

Two grizzlies were removed from the population after repeated conflicts with people, and there were two human injuries (both associated with hunting) in Montana. In late August, a hiker was injured by a grizzly bear after his hiking group followed tracks into a forested area only to stumble upon a sow grizzly with her two cubs that were day-bedded. The man started running and was mauled by the sow before she fled with her cubs. The man survived the attack.

Montana officials reported that from 1992 to 2002, there were thirteen people injured in grizzly attacks in Montana's portion of the Yellowstone ecosystem, with nearly all attacks involving elk hunters having chance encounters with female grizzlies with cubs.

Things were fairly quiet in terms of bear conflicts in Yellowstone National Park that summer, although Park Service officials worked nearly three hundred bear jams where park visitors stopped to view and photograph grizzlies feeding on natural foods along park roadways. Park rangers stayed with the human crowds, maintaining a distance between people and grizzlies while ensuring the bears did not receive food from humans. Yellowstone's human-habituated bears continued to focus on natural foods and largely ignored the crowds.

Yellowstone recorded two conflicts involving human injuries. In the first case, a

A sow grizzly with her single cub of the year.

woman was jogging alone early one morning in late May when she spotted a bear from the corner of her eye. She immediately stopped and stood still as the bear slowly approached, sniffing her fingers. When the bear "very gently" reached out to clamp its teeth down on her thigh, she yelled and squirted the bear in the face with her water bottle. The bear released her leg and slowly walked away.

In early September, two hikers encountered a sow with three young cubs. The bear charged, and the men played dead, but the sow bit one of the men in the leg before picking him up, shaking him, and then releasing him to concentrate on his hiking partner. The hiking partner was able to deploy bear spray in the sow's face, causing the sow and her cubs to flee the area. The man who had been attacked recovered from the puncture wounds to his leg and his fractured fibula.

When the WG&F approved its state management plan for grizzlies in early 2002, it was accompanied by a map showing the outer boundary where grizzlies would be naturally allowed to disperse—including the towns of Farson, Lander, Pinedale, Kemmerer, and Shoshoni at its southern borders. The WG&F plan would not allow grizzlies to occupy areas outside this zone that encompassed all of western Wyoming. In tandem with the WG&F's grizzly plan, the US Forest Service proposed to expand food storage requirements on lands both within the recovery zone, and a large area outside the zone encompassing the Wind River and Wyoming Range mountains—and the new requirements were set to take effect in just a few weeks.

The US Forest Service proposal to greatly expand the area covered by food storage orders was met with stiff opposition.

Return of the Grizzly

Having both the WG&F grizzly plan and the federal food storage proposal under public consideration at the same time proved to be a mistake. Fremont County Commissioners met in early March with Forest Service and WG&F officials in front of a standing-room-only crowd who did not support the plans. As more people arrived, the meeting was moved into a larger court-room, and still the audience overflowed into nearby hallways. After spending two hours discussing the topic and hearing from the audience, the commissioners unanimously passed resolutions that "prohibit the presence, introduction, or reintroduction" of either gray wolves or grizzly bears within the boundaries of the county. In separate resolutions, the commission declared both of these federally protected species to be "unacceptable species" that pose a threat to "public health, safety and livelihood" of the citizens of the county.[65] In addition, the commission passed a resolution opposing and prohibiting the US Forest Service from implementing new food storage requirements within the boundaries of the county. Agency officials were stunned at the turn of events, and there were more coming.

By the next week, members of the Sublette County Outfitters Association attended the Sublette County Commission meeting to discuss the grizzly bear proposals, and the end result was the commission first agreeing to request the Forest Service rescind the proposed food storage order, but later the commission also enacted a somewhat similar resolution to Fremont County's that declared grizzlies "unacceptable" in Sublette County.[66] A local outfitter noted that under the food storage order proposal, having an empty soda can in the back of a pickup truck could earn a person a violation citation, and another noted that the specifics of the order that were designed to deter grizzlies could result in increases in conflicts with black bears. Operating without food storage orders, most outfitters were already using three-strand electric fences and packs of dogs to protect their camps, but the new order would require meat poles to be located away from camps, so they wouldn't be guarded.

Sublette County Commissioner Bill Cramer expressed his view that much of what was happening with management of big predators wasn't driven so much by concern for the species, but more from desires to eliminate other users of national forests.

"I don't blame the wolves or the grizzly bears for being what they are," Cramer said, adding that local governments are "upset, fed up with having things crammed down our throats" and in having local views "being perceived as insignificant. People here are being treated as though they don't matter."

Opposition to the federal proposal continued to grow, and a few days later, a public meeting in Afton, Wyoming drew nearly four hundred outraged residents. Town councils in Afton, Dubois, and Lander threw their weight behind the Fremont County Commission, as did the Lincoln County Commission.[67] The Forest Service heard the message loud and clear, with both Bridger-Teton and Shoshone forest officials quickly deciding to delay action, while also pledging to shrink the size of the area covered by the food storage order. Agency officials agreed to work with local communities in modifying the food storage order to address local concerns.

Part of the reason for the controversy appeared to be that as Wyoming prepared to manage grizzlies without the constraints of federal protection, wildlife managers were imposing more—not less—regulation.

A sow grizzly and her two yearlings.

While the food storage order was blowing up on the Forest Service, the Green River Valley cattlemen had finally had a chance to review the WG&F's grizzly management plan. After that review, a contingent from the association attended the Sublette County Commission meeting to let the commissioners know that the newly approved plan "has led to a plan in which Sublette County's citizens had virtually no voice in determining where grizzlies should or should not exist within the county," and provided even less protection to livestock producers than provisions already in effect, while the species was federally protected.[68] Rancher Albert Sommers led the cattlemen's contingent to the commission meeting, noting that although his cattle herd had suffered losses to grizzlies in the Upper Green for the past decade (losses that doubled dur-

ing that time period), and he'd served on the tri-state committee to examine the federal grizzly conservation strategy, this was the first time that he had ever been granted the opportunity to speak on the issue in his home county at a public forum, because the public hearing process always excluded Sublette County—an area known to harbor grizzly bears, and the site of numerous conflicts every year. He asked the commission to consider the following questions:

- Is it acceptable to have grizzlies at Fremont Lake (a major recreational site a few miles outside of Pinedale) and at the Boy Scout and Girl Scout camps within the county?
- Is it okay for the last migratory sheep flocks in the Wyoming Range to "go away" because grizzlies are allowed

Return of the Grizzly

to increase their range and density to inhabit this mountain range?

- Should elk herds be allowed to be decimated because wolves run them off their feedgrounds, placing the animals in smaller areas at lower elevations in conflict with cattle?
- Should the livestock industry survive in Sublette County?

Cattleman Charles Price, who served on the citizen committee that helped craft the state plan, noted that when WG&F held meetings to discuss the plan, the meetings were held in Casper, Sheridan, and Gillette (communities in the eastern portion of the state, which were without grizzlies) and in Jackson, but never in Sublette County.

The commission noted that by declaring that Sublette County was "economically and socially unacceptable" for grizzlies, they were trying to get a message out to federal and state officials to start listening to the concerns of the people who live with these large predators. Fully a decade after these western counties enacted the resolutions (which were not enforceable regulations or ordinances), environmental groups would cite these resolutions as justification why grizzly bears should remain under federal protection—to protect them from hostile local government officials.

Realizing the problem resulted from lack of involvement of county officials, the IGBC instructed its Yellowstone Ecosystem Subcommittee to invite commissioners to attend their spring meeting in Bozeman, Montana. Agency turmoil continued, as the director of WG&F resigned just a few weeks after county officials began raising an uproar about the plans allowing grizzly presence within their borders. The public spotlight had turned on whether the WG&F had a double standard when it came to keeping attractants away from bears, since it supported the food storage order for forest users. However, photographs had emerged showing dead elk that had been piled up, as well as scattered carcasses from dozens of dead (wolf-killed) elk on one of its elk feedgrounds located inside the grizzly bear recovery zone and surrounded by an area of the national forest where the food storage order was already in place. Overturned and dented garbage cans, and both burned and unburned garbage were also shown at the scene.[69] It was an embarrassment to the department, which vowed to clean up its act as well.

Meanwhile, Sublette County Commissioner Betty Fear teamed up with Upper Green cattleman Albert Sommers to draft a multi-county letter requesting the WG&F withdraw its state grizzly bear management plan. Although they received support from most counties in western Wyoming where grizzlies already had a presence, they failed to convince the WG&F Commission to go back to the drawing board. WG&F commissioners insisted that the state plan was just part of a larger effort that should result in grizzly delisting, and that more input would be solicited when the state established its bear management units and population targets.[70]

Amid this mess, Bureau of Land Management officials announced that due to continued drought, they were cutting back on the number of livestock allowed to graze public lands to no more that 75 percent of the grazing use authorized in their permits, but stockmen were already reducing their herds to an even greater extent. Wildfires once again broke out throughout western Wyoming. Things were rough on the western range.

A yearling grizzly bear in the Yellowstone ecosystem.

Riders for the Upper Green River Cattle Association counted at least thirteen grizzlies in the Upper Green during the 2002 summer grazing season, including at least three sows with cubs. Cattle herds were feeling the impact.[71] Association rider Bob Klaren noted that the impact of a predator attack on a cattle herd is far more than just the dead and injured cattle.

"It keeps the cattle so stirred up, they're not gaining weight like they should," Klaren said, adding that when attack occurs, the cattle act "spooky" and this makes them harder to manage as herd members remember where attacks occur and refuse to move back into those areas. Instead, they start walking fences, looking for a way out.

A grizzly bear was killed in the Deadman Mountain area of the Wyoming Range on Sunday, August 11, 2002—the first official agency confirmation of a grizzly in the Wyoming Range in about a decade.[72] It occurred within the boundary of the Greys River Ranger District of the Bridger-Teton National Forest in northern Lincoln County, and which some claimed was "some thirty miles south" of the current documented grizzly bear range.

Wildlife Services State Director Rod Krischke reported that a private individual, a houndsman with his hounds, had accompanied a USDA Wildlife Services trapper into the area in an attempt to control a bear that had been preying on sheep in the region. "They thought they were pursuing, trailing a black bear," Krischke said, that had left ten domestic sheep dead.

The hounds had run ahead after the bear, and when the two men arrived to the location where the hounds were holding the bear

Return of the Grizzly

in deep deadfall, the houndsman called to his dogs, only to have the bear charge him.

"He just had to react," Krischke said, "at very close range, ten to fifteen feet."

The houndsman reportedly shot the bear, leaving the older adult grizzly male dead. A Wildlife Services official confirmed that the animal was a grizzly, proving that the Wyoming Range did indeed harbor at least one of the federally protected bruins. Matt Mead, then United States Attorney (later Wyoming's governor), declined to prosecute the houndsman, noting that the bear was coming at the man when he shot it, it was a problem bear, and the houndsman wasn't acting alone when he shot the bear since he was accompanying federal officials in attempting to resolve a conflict situation.

Wyoming Game and Fish Department investigator Fred Herbel confirmed that the adult male grizzly killed in the Wyoming Range was known to the agency from years past. In 1999, the bear was captured as a subadult in the Buffalo Valley area as a research bear and radio collared. The agency lost contact with the bear in 2001.

WG&F bear management officer Brian DeBolt said that within the last decade, his agency confirmed the presence of a grizzly as far south as the Hoback Rim, which is about a dozen miles north and about twenty-five miles east of the Deadman Mountain area.

"We've had reports of grizzly bears in the Wyoming Range and suspected they were there, but this is the first confirmed documentation of a grizzly bear there," said WG&F biologist Ron Grogan in a press release issued by the agency.

As federal and state agencies moved forward with plans to delist grizzlies, the population continued to expand.

"The Wyoming Range has good bear habitat and there will likely be more grizzly bears moving into this country in the future," said Grogan. The newly adopted state Grizzly Bear Management Plan called for grizzlies to occupy the Wyoming Range, but WG&F noted in its press release that state plan wouldn't take effect until the grizzly was removed from federal protection.

In late August that year, a sow grizzly and her three yearling cubs were documented as they visited campsites and dug up the remains of burned garbage in the northern Jackson region.

In March 2003, the Wyoming Game and Fish Department issued a press release indicating that a significant step was taken toward state management of grizzly bears with its signing onto the federal grizzly bear conservation strategy, the umbrella document that would guide grizzly bear management in the tri-state Yellowstone region once grizzlies were removed from federal protection under the Endangered Species Act.

"With the official approval of each state in the Yellowstone area, the process has taken a significant step in the quest to return grizzly bear management to Wyoming, Idaho, and Montana," said WG&F Director Brent Manning. With this step, Manning said the groundwork was laid for the US Fish and Wildlife Service to prepare the status change package to remove the grizzly bear from the threatened species list. The conservation strategy would satisfy the FWS's need for "adequate regulatory mechanisms" in order for the delisting process to move forward. Soon after the signing, the complete conservation strategy was slated to be released to the public. The public then learned that the WG&F had signed onto a plan for managing grizzly bears upon removal from federal protection that was more stringent than the provisions of the existing federal recovery plan, and included new population goals for grizzlies in Wyoming.

Before detailing the new provisions, it's worthwhile to look back at what exactly the federal government had required. The federal Grizzly Bear Recovery Plan outlined what it would take to achieve grizzly recovery in the 9,209-square-mile Yellowstone recovery zone, including at least fifteen females with cubs over a running six-year average both inside the recovery zone and within a ten-mile area immediately surrounding the recovery zone; sixteen of eighteen bear management units occupied by females with young; and known, human-caused mortality not to exceed four percent of the population estimate based on the most recent three-year sum of females with cubs. The plan noted, "The target of at least fifteen unduplicated females with cubs indicates a minimum population average of at least 158 bears."

It's important to note that grizzly bear activity in the Upper Green River region was not included in the official counts for achieving grizzly recovery, since the area is about twenty-five miles outside the recovery zone. So neither females with cubs, nor human-caused mortality in the Upper Green, were included in assessing whether the recovery criteria was being met. The reasoning behind this is fairly simple. The recovery plan noted that the designated recovery zone includes "an area large enough and of sufficient habitat quality to support a recovered grizzly bear population."

All of the population parameters described in the recovery plan for the Yellowstone recovery zone had been met by

The recovery plan called for fifteen sows with cubs throughout the ecosystem.

1999 and the population continued to exceed the goals set forth in the plan.

But the conservation strategy included standards not included in the recovery plan, including an overall population goal of five hundred grizzlies in the Yellowstone population. The population estimate for the Yellowstone area was 531 animals, according to WG&F's John Emmerich. Although the recovery plan didn't include an overall numerical population goal, the plan did include a provision for a minimum of 158 bears.

Emmerich pointed out that the recovery plan hadn't address genetic issues, and research demonstrated that to address the genetic health of the population a minimum population of four hundred bears was needed. To provide some leeway, the strategy placed the goal at five hundred bears.

In addition, all monitoring and population counts would be done throughout the Yellowstone region, not just in the existing recovery zone. That meant the grizzlies in the Upper Green, and the management removals resulting from conflicts with those grizzlies, would be counted. The strategy stated, "This is more stringent than the system under the recovery plan and allows management of the entire population. . . ."

Emmerich said the WG&F Commission approved a state management plan for grizzly bears that drew an exterior boundary line for grizzly bear occupancy, but his agency would begin a public process to determine what bear distribution and numbers would be inside that line. That process would be the state's determination of what areas are "biologically suitable and socially acceptable" for grizzlies.

The strategy document stated that the intent of the strategy "is to allow grizzlies to expand their range and numbers and reoccupy all biologically suitable and socially acceptable habitats."

With the continued expansion of the grizzly population into new range, US Forest Service officials spent most of 2003 working toward expansion of food storage orders for recreationalists in the Shoshone and Bridger-Teton National Forests. Food storage requirements had already been in place within the grizzly bear recovery zone, but the proposal would expand the order to encompass national forest lands outside the zone, such as down the Wind River and Wyoming Range mountains. The proposal was met with strong opposition, and the agency bungled the process by first threatening to rush the order through, not addressing significant issues posed by the order (such as how to hang food in trees when one was camped above timberline), and failing to hold public meetings so citizen concerns could be discussed. Forest officials met repeatedly with community officials to address public concerns while installing needed infrastructure, including meat poles, for the program and providing food boxes for those who voluntarily wanted to comply. But these actions weren't enough because the federal agency continued to handle the issue badly.

Local communities continued to balk at the new food storage requirements. After hearing testimony from county residents for more than an hour at a meeting in June 2003, the Fremont County Commission once again enacted a resolution expressing opposition to a proposed Shoshone National Forest food storage order which had been re-drafted and given the title of "occupancy and use restrictions." The order was slated to be in effect from March 1 through December 1 annually and addressed possessing, storing, and transporting food, refuse, animals, and animal parts, as well as camping.

Among other provisions, the proposal required that an unattended big-game carcass be at least two hundred yards from a national forest system trail and prohibited knowingly camping within a half-mile of an animal carcass. The order required that all food, refuse, and harvested animal carcasses must be "acceptably stored or acceptably possessed."

Exemptions to the order included "persons with a permit issued by the Forest Supervisor specifically exempting them," those placing black bear baits for hunts, and federal and state wildlife officials placing baits for research or management purposes.

The newly adopted Fremont County resolution cited threats to the health, safety, and livelihoods to the citizens of Fremont County and opposed the Forest Service's efforts to implement the proposal within the boundaries of the county. When the food storage order appeared on the county commission's agenda, the public responded. It was an overflowing commission meeting room at the courthouse in Lander, and of the two dozen residents who spoke, all expressed opposition to the resolution, with the exception of a National Outdoor Leadership School representative who did not state an official position on the issue. Forest Service officials did not attend the hearing, which was recorded by the commission.

Fremont County Commission Chairman Doug Thompson said after the last ruckus over the proposed expansion of the order to encompass all of the Wind River Mountain range, Forest Service officials pledged to meet with those concerned and address the specific problems with the order.

"That was not done," Thompson stated. That the Forest Service hadn't held public meetings or hearings was a recurring theme in the complaints voiced at the hearing from both commissioners and residents alike. Commissioner Crosby Allen characterized the revised order as "basically a metamorphosed document of the original one," with few changes. "It's the same horse," Allen said.

Rancher Jim Sloan said, "What part of 'no' does the Forest Service not understand? The citizens of Fremont County spoke loudly" the year prior when the issue arose. Tom Adams, representing the City of Lander, said the municipality remained opposed to the food storage order, adding that local governments hadn't been contacted by forest officials in attempt to resolve the city's problems with the proposal. Adams said the new proposal "appears more convoluted than last year's" and requested the commission maintain its opposition.

Ron Cunningham of the Fremont County Youth Camp spoke in opposition to the order. "If one of our campers were to leave an empty candy wrapper, we would be liable for that," Cunningham said.

Lander Llama Company owner Scott Woodruff said, "I firmly believe this is about liability and deep pockets." Woodruff said the bear-proof containers required by the order are expensive and not justified in the southern portion of the Winds.

The year prior, the National Outdoor Leadership School (NOLs) had sent a letter of opposition to the proposal, according to NOLS's John Gookin. But forest officials had been working with his organization to try to address its concerns.

After listening to testimony, Commis-sioner Allen said he felt even more strongly opposed to the proposal. Commissioner Lanny Applegate noted that it was his understanding the Forest Service would hold public meetings, but had failed to do so. Applegate also questioned what federal officials marked up as conflicts, when in reality the conflicts were nothing more than bear sightings. Thompson agreed, stating, "That a sighting is a conflict is a contrived issue."

"Is this draft to manage the people, or manage the bear?" Applegate questioned.

Faced with continued opposition, the Forest Service once again chose to delay, finally signing the order near the end of 2003, and to take effect the next spring. Opposition quieted when the public learned that the area covered had shrunk substantially from what had originally been proposed. The new order expanded food storage requirements only to those areas of the forests where grizzly bears were currently known to exist or could reasonably be expected to occur and included recognizable geographic features to help forest users comply with the order. Dropped from the final order was the southern portion of the Wind River Range on the Pinedale Ranger District, the entire Wyoming and Salt River Ranges on the Greys River and Kemmerer Ranger Districts, and the southern portion of the Big Piney Ranger District. In addition, the forests had made infrastructure improvements to help the public comply with the order, including the installation of equipment in campgrounds and the backcountry such as bear-resistant food storage boxes, garbage containers, and hanging poles. Bearproof equipment such as panniers and backpacker tubes were also made available for loan from Forest Service district offices.

Rancher Albert Sommers moves a Hereford bull.

In early July 2003, a grizzly bear killed four beef calves in five days in the Upper Green, and a four-hundred-pound adult male grizzly was trapped and relocated from the area in response. A second bear that continued preying on livestock evaded capture efforts. By late July, there were thirteen confirmed grizzly bear depredations, compared to only twelve in the prior year's grazing season.[73] One of the kills involved three calves within about 250 yards of each other. One calf was still alive and had to be destroyed. WG&F's Mark Bruscino said, "We rarely, rarely see what's called surplus killing with bears, except with sheep. That was unusual. I have seen it only once or twice before in my whole career." An adult male grizzly was live-trapped on site and released east of Yellowstone National Park. By mid-August, the number of dead cattle

increased to twenty-two. A small female grizzly with two cubs of the year was captured and released on site since there was no evidence linking the adult bear to the livestock killing. Another adult male grizzly was captured and relocated out of the area. Although still under federal protection, since grizzlies are classified as a trophy game species, WG&F would have to compensate ranchers for verified losses to this species. Before the end of the month, a few more cattle were confirmed as grizzly kills in the Upper Green, and a grizzly had killed ten sheep in the area as well.

Bears and wolves seemed to have increasing interactions, with both species vying for animal carcasses. Neck snares set to catch depredating wolves in the Sunlight Basin managed to catch and kill a yearling grizzly. Federal authorities thereafter discontinued

Return of the Grizzly

the use of wolf neck snares in grizzly bear range.

Under pressure from environmental groups to take a hard look at continued cattle grazing in the Upper Green, the US Forest Service released a draft environmental impact statement for continued livestock grazing on the Upper Green allotment, and although the allotment is the single largest allotment in the national forest system, there were only seventeen letters of public comment. Environmental groups had heavy criticism of the federal agency for continuing to allow grazing in the face of conflicts with wolves and grizzlies, but the cattlemen were surprised that the Forest Service failed to acknowledge their good land stewardship. In his letter to the agency, cattleman Albert Sommers wrote: "Over the years, when concerns have arisen about cattle impacts to the resource, the Upper Green River Cattle Association has worked diligently to solve the problems. We have hired additional riders, tried electric fencing, developed a monitoring program, reduced numbers in drought, moved cattle off the allotment early, and tried different grazing regimes. We have conducted these management options with the help of the Forest Service, but rarely at its insistence. . . . We have accomplished or exceeded nearly every expectation the Forest Service has had for our allotment."

The Forest Service issued its decision on the grazing project, appeals were filed, and the federal agency then withdrew its decision, stating that there were issues raised during the appeal that needed further consideration. The Greater Yellowstone Coalition and the Wyoming Outdoor Council had teamed up in their appeal to request the Forest Service consider requiring twenty-four-hour supervision of livestock by peo-ple, electric fencing of livestock at night, and a change to steers-only, rather than allowing mother cows with calves on the allotment. The appeal also suggested that the Forest Service must consider prohibiting predator control actions by state or federal officials "for the purpose of removing any predators to benefit or protect domestic livestock on forest lands."

While the cattlemen were going rounds with government officials and environmental groups behind desks, grizzlies continued to impact their herds. Five grizzlies were removed from the Upper Green by mid-July, including one adult male that had a prior history of livestock depredations in the Cody area, who was relocated the year prior, and moved into the Upper Green where it continued its stock-killing ways, killing three calves in three nights. This bear was removed from the population, but the other four grizzlies (two males and two females) were relocated to other parts of the ecosystem after being trapped at livestock depredation sites in the Upper Green.

As the summer continued, more cattle kills were tallied, and more bears were relocated out of the area. Other bears preyed on the Thoman family's sheep flocks. In one case, the flock was in an inaccessible area, so herders moved the flock and set up a new night pen in an attempt to get relief from the depredations.

By the end of the grazing season, the cattlemen had tallied 186 head of missing calves (from all causes) and confirmed losses to grizzlies included one cow, twenty-four calves, and six yearlings. WG&F compensates the market value of 3.5 calves for every confirmed calf kill, provided there are other missing calves. The formula was established in recognition that there are calf kills that can't be found for verification, and was designed to ensure that a stockman couldn't be compensated for more calves than were missing.

The losses to the cattle producers totaled 6.9 percent, up from the historic rate of 2 percent. According to information compiled by the UGRCA, the total calf loss due to grizzly depredation from 1995–2004 was estimated to be a minimum of 520 calves, with a financial impact of $260,000. But compensation was provided for only 235 calves, with a market value of $117,500. The cattlemen had been reimbursed for less than half the calves they believe were lost to grizzlies.

Meanwhile, WG&F moved forward with its proposal for "grizzly bear occupancy" in Wyoming, a fine-tuning from its state bear management plan. The plan resulted in Sublette and Fremont county officials renewing their declarations that their counties were not "socially acceptable" grizzly bear habitat.

Hoping that the WG&F proposal was another necessary step toward delisting grizzlies, the Hot Springs County Board of County Commissioners did not oppose the occupancy document, but submitted a detailed letter of comment to the state wildlife agency, outlining some of the basic problems Wyoming residents had with all the planning for grizzlies. It stated: "While it may seem trite, regardless of viewpoint regarding the degree to which grizzly bears and humans can co-exist, there are no conflicts, property damage or injuries due to grizzly bears where there are no grizzly bears. Conversely, conflicts occur where humans and grizzly bears occupy the same area. If territory occupied by grizzly bears expands, then more and more bears will occupy privately owned or operated lands, and conflicts on those lands will increase . . .

Since conflict cannot be totally avoided, it will be necessary to minimize the area where bears and humans are forced to coexist. The bears have been given considerable primacy within the {recovery zone}."

The commission wrote:

The term "socially acceptable" needs to be defined by more than the visceral "we don't want 'em" that some of our constituents have communicated. In order to be 'socially acceptable' the grizzly bear and its management must not infringe on the constitutional rights of the county, its citizens, and other human beings. We hold that the needs of a grizzly bear population are secondary to mankind. Delisting from protection under the Endangered Species Act supports that position. The human population must be healthy in order to apply its husbandry to the bear. Our citizens must be able to earn a living, recreate, and live in safety and security from harm or danger. Our citizens have the right to be free from the threat of harm or danger.

The letter continued:

As a society, we have promulgated laws and we enforce penalties on lawbreakers. We have laws that protect persons from being threatened by others. The plethora of grizzly bear facts and statistics published since 2000 demonstrate that where the grizzly bear ranges there is an expectation of property damage and injury to people. The threat is universal and ubiquitous. Wherever within our physical jurisdiction the presence of the grizzly bear carries the threat of harm or damage to the health, safety, or general welfare, including the right and ability to earn a living from public lands, then the grizzly bear is not socially acceptable.

The commission's letter also detailed the negative economic impact expected to the local economy from grizzly bear occupancy, as well as concern for other wildlife populations, should management decisions continue to favor grizzlies over other uses, even after delisting occurs, as the county feared will occur.

The commission expressed concern for the burden put on livestock producers, when there are a variety of costs associated with bear damage that is not compensated. The letter stated, "To impose these costs on the human population beyond what is absolutely necessary to keep the grizzly bear from being re-listed is arguably an unwarranted burden on the populace."

Although WG&F's proposal called for limiting grizzly occupancy on private land, the Hot Springs County board noted, "a parallel position to protect the rights of users of public lands outside the primary conservation area has not been made. We argue that coexistence of grizzly bears and humans cannot be without conflict and that these conflicts will severely hamper the quality of life and economic well-being of those who use public lands outside the [recovery zone]. The defining elements of 'socially acceptable' are not limited only to private lands but extend to public multiple use lands."

After evaluating extensive public input received during a four-month process, WG&F released its final plan for grizzly bear occupancy.

The document first defined biologically suitable habitat based on grizzly bear ecological indicators:

A grizzly sow with two yearling grizzlies.

Human uses, including livestock grazing, timber harvest, oil and gas development, areas of high road densities and recreational activities/developed sites create potential increases for human/grizzly bear conflicts and increasing potential for bear mortalities. Areas supporting these human uses are considered socially unacceptable for grizzly bear occupancy. These areas were mapped and compared to the biologically suitable habitat base to determine those areas in northwest Wyoming most suited for grizzly occupancy.

The plan, entitled "Wyoming Grizzly Bear Occupancy Management Guidelines," outlined areas considered suitable for grizzly bear occupancy. The state agency had received more than seventeen thousand written comments from the public—more than the department received on any other issue in its history.

"The comments ranged widely from those who want grizzly bears confined to Yellowstone Park to those who would like to see bears in every corner of the state," said WG&F Director Terry Cleveland. "We have been working with the US Fish and Wildlife Service to ensure our grizzly bear occupancy proposal will meet federal requirements for delisting. The plan includes modifications based on public input. The result is a plan that addresses as much of the public concern as possible while still meeting minimum requirements for removal of bears from the endangered species list."

"Approval of this grizzly bear occupancy proposal will be essential in demonstrating Wyoming's commitment to moving the delisting process forward," said Cleveland. "It's time to move on to delisting, to return grizzly bears to state management control, and to stabilize the bear population in Wyoming. Following delisting, Wyoming is committed to managing for a stable bear population while assuring a fully recovered population of bears is maintained."

The final guidelines determined that "the biologically suitable and socially acceptable habitats . . . occur north of the Snake River Canyon and Hoback River, which includes a contiguous region bounding the Absaroka Range and that portion of the Wind River Range north of Boulder Creek."

The agency determined that the majority of the Wyoming and Salt River Ranges are not suited for grizzly bear occupancy due to a combination of factors, nor is the Wind River Range south of Boulder Creek.

"Additionally, all private lands and most of the lands managed by the Bureau of Land Management outside the National Forests have high potential for human/grizzly bear conflicts and a source of grizzly bear mortality making them unsuitable for sustaining grizzly bears," the plan stated.

The Upper Green, with its yearly conflicts between grizzlies and livestock, was specifically addressed in the final version of the plan. WG&F wrote:

Based on current road densities, presence of domestic sheep and current levels of conflict with livestock, the Upper Green River area on Forest could also be considered unsuitable for grizzly bear occupancy. However, important biological issues make the Upper Green River area very important in ensuring Conservation Strategy population and distribution objectives will be met long-term. The Upper Green River area is presently occupied by grizzly bears and is important contiguous habitat that links the bear population between the Gros Ventre/Upper Hoback area, Upper Wind River Range, and core bear habitat north of this area. Recognizing the significance of this area for bear movements is important, but this does not preclude managing for low bear densities, if needed . . . to minimize conflicts.

WG&F maintained that the current grizzly distribution in the Yellowstone region needed to be maintained to assure the minimum acceptable population threshold is maintained. The plan further stated, "The combination of the proposed geographic area and management strategies outlined in this plan should provide a sufficient amount of habitat in Wyoming to adequately support Wyoming's share of the tristate Yellowstone population."

"Bears do not recognize jurisdictional boundaries," according to the plan. "Some grizzly bears will move into areas considered socially unsuitable for grizzly bear occupancy. The Department cannot realistically implement a management program that is designed to immediately remove every grizzly bear that moves outside of suitable habitat. Unless conflicts occur, the presence of these bears may go undetected for some time. If a bear is involved in a conflict, the Department will remove the offending individual."

The plan continued: "There are large blocks of public and private land outside of the primary conservation area that are not suitable for grizzly bear occupancy. Grizzly bear dispersal and occupancy will be discouraged in these areas. There are other areas outside of the PCA where the potential for human-bear conflicts will require that grizzly bears be managed for low numbers depending on localized situations."

Encounters with grizzlies on rural roads had become expected in some areas.

Public Fracas

For the portion of the Wind River Range south of Boulder Creek and all private and BLM lands adjacent to the National Forests with high potential for human/grizzly conflicts, these areas "will be managed to discourage grizzly bears from dispersing to, and occupying these areas due to the potential for human/bear conflicts and bear mortalities." WG&F added that "total exclusion of grizzly bears in this area is probably not possible, as portions of this area provide biologically suitable habitat for bears and it is contiguous with occupied habitat."

In November 2005, FWS issued rules designating the population of grizzly bears in the Yellowstone ecosystem as a "distinct population segment" and proposed to remove this population of bears from federal protection. US Senators from Wyoming Craig Thomas and Mike Enzi were on hand in Washington, DC, to join US Interior Secretary Gale Norton and Fish and Wildlife Service Director Dale Hall in announcing the delisting proposal, as were state wildlife officials from the region.

Hall called the event "an important milestone in conservation," and Norton said grizzly bear recovery is an "extraordinary accomplishment," given that recovery efforts began only after the species had plummeting toward extinction.

"This great icon of the American West has a promising future," Norton said. Norton's speech emphasized the "cooperative conservation" between numerous agencies and organizations that led to bear recovery. Wyoming's comprehensive bear monitoring and fulltime staff devoted to bear management were noted in Norton's speech.

"The sum of all of these efforts brought us where we are today," Norton said. "We have worked together and we have succeeded."

Enzi invited those attending and watching the press conference via satellite to visit Wyoming and Yellowstone National Park, adding he hoped visitors may get a glimpse of the great bear, but hoped they wouldn't have any bear encounters. Enzi pointed out that a grizzly is not just a symbol, but a flesh-and-blood animal that roams Wyoming. He pointed to the tall fence encasing the elementary school grounds in Wapiti as an example of Wyoming's residents living with grizzlies.

Reaction was mixed. Environmental groups warned of the dire consequences of delisting, while political representatives in the region praised the success of grizzly bear recovery.

Louisa Willcox of the Natural Resources Defense Council said: "Federal protection is the only reason these bears exist in Yellowstone today, and they aren't yet ready to survive without it. . . . We would love to see grizzlies taken off the Endangered Species list when they're ready. But that can't happen if the laws protecting grizzlies are weakened, and if they lose the few remaining scraps of land that support them. When those scraps are gone, neither the bears nor the wild land will be there for future generations."

Wyoming Governor Dave Freudenthal had the opposite view. He said:

If the draft rule becomes final and the bear is de-listed, I sense that the fear and hostility that is currently building in Wyoming will ease, leading to not only a better day for those who live with the bear, but also for the bear itself. However, if the de-listing rule is challenged or is otherwise derailed, I am afraid that the presently intensifying rate of bear-human conflict will only escalate, leading to more fear, more hostility and, in the end, more bear and potentially human mortality—a course which is nothing but counterproductive.

As part of the delisting process, FWS put forth several new major documents as amendments to the grizzly bear recovery plan. A conservation strategy would guide post-delisting management of the grizzly bear in the Greater Yellowstone Area. The official conservation strategy redesignated the 9,210-square-mile recovery zone as the Primary Conservation Area (PCA), which was to serve as a secure area for grizzly bears, with population and habitat conditions that allowed the grizzly bear population to achieve recovery and expand outside the PCA. Outside the PCA, grizzlies "will be allowed to expand into biologically suitable and socially acceptable areas."[74] These are areas "that are not managed solely for bears but in which their needs are considered along with other uses." Habitat standards included in the Conservation Strategy would apply only inside the PCA, which encompasses more than half of all suitable habitat for grizzlies within the Yellowstone region. All bear removals in the Yellowstone region, both inside and outside the PCA, must be consistent with the strategy's mortality limits.

A separate document detailed genetic monitoring information, while another served as a habitat-based recovery criteria amendment to the recovery plan, providing for maintenance of secure habitat through management of motorized access routes and development sites, prohibiting new livestock grazing allotments within the recovery zone above the 1998 baseline, and requiring ongoing monitoring of four major food sources: whitebark pine, ungulates, cutthroat trout, and army cutworm moths.

Also included was revised methodologies for calculating total population size, known-to-unknown mortality ratios, and sustainable mortality limits for the Yellowstone grizzly bear population. As part of its revision to the recovery plan, FWS expanded the area in which the demographic criteria would be applied to include most of northwest Wyoming and southwestern Montana.

When WG&F examined the delisting proposal, the agency realized there were unresolved issues between the state plans and the federal proposal: the delisting rule included about 8,800 square miles of "suitable habitat," including the Wind River Range, outside the current grizzly bear recovery zone, but with the exception of domestic sheep allotments on the western edge of the range.

The final rule noted, "Management decisions on US Forest Service lands will continue to consider potential impacts on grizzly bear habitat and will be managed so as to allow grizzly bear expansion in terms of numbers and distribution."

In contrast, the state bear occupancy plan stated, "There are large blocks of public and private land outside of (the current recovery zone) that are not suitable for grizzly bear occupancy. Grizzly bear dispersal and occupancy will be discouraged in these areas."

While that might be WG&F's intention, FWS's proposed rule noted, "Although state management plans apply to all suitable habitat outside the primary conservation area, habitat management on public lands is directed by federal land management plans, not state management plans."

At the same time delisting was moving forward, the US Forest Service finalized forest plan amendments for grizzly bear conservation for the national forests in the

Yellowstone region, and each of the three states adopted their own state grizzly bear management plans.

With all components finally in place for removing grizzly bears from the threatened species list, FWS moved forward with delisting in March 2007, officially removing bears from federal protection. As expected, litigation soon followed, but other events were unfolding on the ground

In May 2007, Jim Cole, a Montana wildlife photographer, was hiking alone off-trail in Yellowstone's Hayden Valley when he was mauled by a sow bear that was accompanied by a young cub.[75] Cole survived the attack with severe wounds to his face. Cole is the author of several books about grizzly bears, and had also survived a mauling by a grizzly bear in Glacier National Park fourteen years prior. Cole had previously been ticketed by Yellowstone officials for intentionally getting too close to bears in the park in his photography pursuits, but was later acquitted of the charge.

In another instance, a few months after grizzlies were delisted, a Wyoming black bear hunter mistakenly killed a grizzly bear in the southern Wind River Mountains— the southernmost documentation of grizzly bear presence in Wyoming in decades. The man received a citation for taking a trophy game animal out of season.

While grizzly bear recovery was being argued in a federal courtroom, bear managers wrote in *Yellowstone Science* in 2008:

> As the population of grizzly bears expanded in the ecosystem, bear density inside Yellowstone National Park

While wildlife managers celebrated grizzly bear recovery, bear advocates headed to court to reinstitute protection for grizzlies.

Return of the Grizzly

also increased. Recent studies suggest that bears inside YNP are probably at carrying capacity, a term used to define the limits of available space, food, and other resources in the environment. As a population approaches this limit, juvenile mortality increases, females tend to initiate breeding later in life, and reproduction tends to decline. The study team has documented a decline in litter size as bear numbers increased, and a higher incidence of starvation and predation of cubs occurred inside YNP.[76]

Led by the Greater Yellowstone Coalition, three separate lawsuits challenging the grizzly bear delisting were filed, and after two years of litigation, a 2009 federal court opinion found that:

- The regulatory mechanisms to protect grizzlies upon delisting were inadequate;
- FWS had failed to adequately consider the impacts of global warming and other factors on whitebark pine production, an important food source for grizzlies.

While FWS appealed the decision to a higher court, in March 2010, FWS reinstituted federal protection for grizzlies in the Yellowstone region. Finally, in 2011, the Ninth Circuit Court of Appeals affirmed the FWS's determination that existing regulatory mechanisms were indeed adequate to protect grizzlies in the Yellowstone area, but ruled that FWS had failed to adequately explain its conclusion that the loss of whitebark pine was not a threat to the population.

The appeals court noted:

Perhaps the Service's delisting process, based on two decades of grizzly population growth, was well underway before the whitebark pine loss problem appeared on the radar and could be studied. But now that this threat has emerged, the Service cannot take a full-speed ahead, damn-the-torpedoes approach to delisting—especially given the ESA's 'policy of institutionalized caution.'[77]

And so it was back to square one, with grizzly bears in the Yellowstone region once again listed as a threatened species under the Endangered Species Act.

CHAPTER 8

THOMAN SHEEP

Domestic sheep flock belonging to the Thoman family graze the Upper Green.

Hearing the sounds of a grizzly bear killing sheep in the darkness outside his camp, the sheepherder grabbed a flashlight and a can of bear pepper spray and raced outside. He jumped on his horse that had been tied nearby and charged the grizzly, letting loose with his can of spray. The herder continued spraying the bear in the face until it fled. It was a dangerous, and ridiculous, position to be in. According to protocol, the herder probably should have stayed within the safe confines of his camp and let the bear continue killing the sheep. But to listen to the killing in the dark, without taking action, hadn't seemed right either.

In May 2002, domestic sheep rancher Mary Thoman called together a brainstorming session of agency officials to discuss how to reduce conflicts between grizzly bears and her family's sheep flocks in the Upper Green.[78] Her family had grazed three bands of sheep (about 1,300 per band) on the Elk Ridge allotment complex from July through

Mary Thoman riding her Upper Green sheep allotment.

September in the Upper Green for more than three decades, far outside the grizzly bear recovery zone. Each flock has its own herder, herding dogs, and livestock guardian dogs, but the region is so remote that help can be days away, and cell service is spotty in the areas where it is even available.

Thoman described the scenario herders faced in tending to her sheep the prior summer when there were up to three grizzly bears preying on her flocks every night. Herders were falling asleep at night only to awaken to the sounds of a grizzly bear mauling sheep. A herder would grab a gun and rush out, firing into the air to scare the bear away. The same event was repeated throughout the night, until sometimes the bears refused to flee. To kill a bear would be to violate federal law, and the herders had been instructed to shoot a

bear only as a last resort to save human life. Thoman pleaded with officials to help the herders find more tools to reduce the risk posed to human life by such regular contact between man and beast. During the session, Thoman was told that other methods were very limited and doomed to eventual failure, but if she wanted to forego her grazing allotments, "incentives" could probably be provided for an agreement to shut down domestic sheep grazing in the region. That was not the solution the Thoman family had been looking for.

Predator losses had risen out of control on the allotments, rising to 490 sheep in one grazing season (220 breeding ewes and 270 lambs), but the Thomans weren't prone to giving up. Thoman persuaded agency officials to agree to designate "safe havens" in her allotments—areas where the sheep

Pedro travels from his native Peru to work as a sheepherder in the Upper Green.

could be held while agencies were trying to deal with problem bears. This was a concession, since national forest managers held the Thomans to strict management protocols which were designed to minimize the impact of sheep grazing. By mid-August that year, two adult male grizzlies were removed from the Thoman's flocks, including one that was euthanized because of its history of previous livestock depredations.[79]

The Thoman family's Elk Ridge Allotment Complex is located twenty-five miles outside the PCA/Recovery Zone, and had thirty-five depredation events by grizzly bears in the previous three years, with 140 dead sheep, and bear managers removing and relocating four bears from the grazing complex. The nearby Upper Green River cattle allotment was another area of chronic depredation, with ninety-five con-

flicts reported in the previous five years, involving the death of eighty-six cattle, and numerous other injuries to cattle during the same time. Eight grizzly bears were captured and relocated in response to the depredations, and seven more had been permanently removed from the population.

After ranch patriarch Bill Thoman died in a tragic accident a few years prior, the Thoman women took over running their family's western range cattle and sheep ranch full time, including sheep grazing in the Upper Green. Bill's daughter Mary took over dealing with agency regulations and personnel. Even though few viable options were put forth to alleviate the conflicts between her family's sheep flocks and grizzlies in the Upper Green, Mary insisted that something could be done and pledged to try out different deterrents. She eventually went

Return of the Grizzly

Supplies are stored in large bear-proof containers.

to the Wyoming Animal Damage Management Board and received funding to purchase electric fences for use as portable night pens on the ranch's mountain grazing allotments. Installation of the night pens wasn't without its problems, as none of the sheep nor their guardian dogs had ever been near an electric fence. Some of the animals received electric shocks, and there were a few stampedes and torn-down fences. But the Thomans persisted, spending many long hours laboring to set up the pens in a manner that would keep their sheep safe.

Eventually, it was a success. Installation of night pens allowed for the sheep and sheepherders to be protected, while reducing the number of grizzly bears removed from the area due to conflict. Importantly, the pens allowed the sheep to calmly rest at night, instead of running from predators.

The result was the family's four-month old lambs were coming off the mountain at a record weight of ninety-six pounds at the end of the grazing season.

One of the Thoman sheep allotments was frequented by twelve grizzly bears and four black bears in 2010, and two black bears were removed by wildlife managers in response to depredations. A second flock was harassed by two grizzly bear sows and their cubs, and two wolves, with one grizzly bear removed by state officials. A third sheep flock had two or three grizzly bears, six wolves, and a mountain lion around it throughout the summer. The sheep were safe at night, but these big predators were successful in preying on the herds in daylight hours.

"The major killing occurred during the daytime when small groups of sheep were

Portable electrified night pens to keep the sheep safe from grizzlies at night.

run up into the timber or rocks and then killed," Mary said. State and federal wildlife managers and animal damage experts were on the scene to help minimize livestock losses and document problems, but losses to predators were substantial. Mary said that the losses would have been "astronomical" without the use of the night pens.

In 2010, predators killed 259 ewes and 186 lambs, with a total value of about $65,000. The Thomans received nearly $54,000 in damage compensation by WG&F, with the ranch forced to absorb the remaining $11,000 loss on its own.

Livestock losses due to large carnivores on the allotments had increased steadily in recent years, with damage ranging from about $17,000 in 2005, to $40,000 in 2008, and 2010's $65,000. Mary said that

while the ranch had made adjustments to try to control losses, the arrival of female grizzlies with cubs resulted in a doubling of livestock losses.

One night in late September, a female grizzly and her cub attempted to dig underneath the electric fence to get to the sheep inside, but failed. The trench left by the digging bruins was an impressive sight.

"With the nightly use of pens, the herders were able to secure the three herds at night and did not have to jeopardize their lives to check on sheep that may have been attacked by bears or wolves," Mary said.

One of the Thoman's sheepherders was mauled by a grizzly bear during the 2009 grazing season when he stepped away from his tent in the middle of the night to check on a barking livestock protection dog. The dog was barking at a sow grizzly with two cubs that had killed a sheep. The sow charged the herder and mauled him. Two of the herders drained cans of pepper spray during the attack which lasted only moments before the bears fled. The mauled herder was severely injured, but did survive the attack.

While the night pens were deemed a success, not all deterrents the Thoman herders tried worked as well. Herders on one allotment used a large spotlight on the back of their tent to discourage grizzly bears, while another used a small electric pen around his sleeping tent. Herders using an air horn to scare bears away found it worked to deter black bears, but actually attracted the curiosity of grizzlies. Flashlights had no deterrent effects at all. Herders had to be moved out of their tent and into a sheep wagon until electric pens could be set up around their campsites once a grizzly threatened to enter the herder camp.

Herders stay in these hard-sided camps as much as possible, but when the flocks are moved too deep into the backcountry, or into the wilderness, they sleep in tents since mechanical transportation is not allowed within the wilderness boundary.

On another occasion, a sow grizzly and her cub became entangled in the electric fence around a herd, gaining entrance and killing about twenty sheep. Thoman feared a repeat performance from this sow: "This bear may acclimate to swatting the pen, as this was the second attempt she made at entering the pen."

At the time, the Thomans were using a variety of non-lethal predator deterrents, including a half-dozen livestock protection dogs with each flock and utilizing bear-proof containers for storage of food and

Food for the flock's guardian dogs is kept in a bear-proof box.

Thoman Sheep

supplies. Herders working for the Thoman ranch are supplied with pepper spray and receive training in safety and food storage requirements.

The Thomans use livestock protection dogs that have proven to be very effective against male grizzlies, but have limited effectiveness with both bear family groups and with wolves. Wolves killed four of the Thoman guardian dogs in the Upper Green in 2004.

Despite the nearly four-fold increase in added expenses and time requirements for tending their sheep on the allotments due to increased predator presence, the Thomans maintain that these four allotments are some of the best in America, producing fat lambs in a pristine environment, and which average ninety pounds at 120 days of age. Mary fears that multiple use management is falling by the wayside on the allotments, with the Endangered Species Act driving management of all resources, and inflexible US Forest Service regulations and officials putting the squeeze on her family's future on the allotments.

The arrival of female grizzlies with cubs resulted in a doubling of livestock losses.

CHAPTER 9

MULTIPLE VICTIMS

Biologists with the IGBST and the National Park Service fit a grizzly bear with a radio collar. Once a bear is radio collared, biologists can track its movements with telemetry. USGS photo Interagency Grizzly Bear Study Team.

The Interagency Grizzly Bear Study Team (IGBST) had been in charge of grizzly bear research for decades, and by the summer of 2010, team members had monitored more than six hundred individual grizzly bears in the previous thirty-five years. The June 2010 field season shouldn't be any different than those in years past. But tragedy would occur, for the first time in IGBST history, that June.

Since late May, a two-man IGBST field crew had been busy setting traps to capture and collar grizzly bears outside Yellowstone National Park in the Shoshone National Forest.[80] The men did their work on horseback, but after several weeks of effort, still hadn't managed to capture a grizzly in the Kitty Creek drainage, even though there were grizzly tracks in the area, and a grizzly had sprung their snares on several occasions. The team's last day in the area was set for June 17, and when the men arrived at their first snare site, they found they had finally succeeded in capturing an adult male grizzly bear, a ten-year-old bear weighing about 430 pounds that had never been captured before. After processing the bear, which they identified as Bear 646, the men pulled their remaining snares and took down their area closure signs since no further trapping would take place. They believed there was no human activity in the area due to conditions one called "spitting snow and cold." In fact, they hadn't encountered any hikers during the three weeks they had been setting and checking snares in the area. When they left the scene around lunchtime, the tranquilized bear was holding his head up and swaying from side to side as the effects of the drug began wearing off.

They rode their horses further up the drainage to find their second trap site also held a bear—this time a four-year-old female grizzly. It was after 5 p.m. when the men finished processing the sow and began the hour-long ride back down the trail. The sow was already on her feet by the time the men pulled the remaining snares and signs and left the scene. The team had nearly reached their truck and trailer parked along the roadway when they were contacted by an elderly woman at a nearby cabin, asking if they had encountered anyone hiking, as her husband was overdue from an anticipated short hike.

Splitting up, the crew leader turned around and headed back up the trail to the first trap site, leaving his partner to contact other bear authorities. Erwin Evert's body was found face down and mauled, about twenty yards from where the team had left Bear 646. DNA evidence on the seventy-year-old victim's body confirmed Bear 646 had killed Mr. Evert, who had hiked about 1,700 feet off the main trail where the bear was recovering from immobilization and was killed in the encounter. Bear 646 was later shot and killed less than two miles from the trap site.

A bear jam in Yellowstone National Park.

Return of the Grizzly

It was a terrible tragedy for all involved, and in the aftermath, the IGBST adopted new procedures aimed at improving public safety by keeping signs up at capture sites for several days after the conclusion of trapping efforts.

The year 2010 was an incredibly demanding one for bear managers throughout the ecosystem, with record-high numbers of human-grizzly conflicts (295) scattered throughout the ecosystem.[81] There weren't many winter-killed ungulate carcasses for bears emerging from their dens, and spring was cold, with a delay in snow melt and the resulting development of bear plant foods. There were few spawning cutthroat trout and whitebark pine seed production was poor. That year, grizzlies turned to feeding on newborn elk calves in spring, and to eating false truffles in fall. More grizzlies damaged property, obtained unnatural foods, killed livestock, and inflicted injuries on humans than the long-term average. In an unprecedented move, in early July the Bridger-Teton National Forest closed much of the high-recreational use area of the Upper Green to overnight camping due to the presence of grizzlies roaming through camps.

Yellowstone park rangers struggled to keep up, dealing with a record high of 435 bear jams along roads inside the park.[82]

In the dark of night on July 28, an adult female grizzly and three yearlings entered the Soda Butte Campground located just a few miles northeast of Yellowstone National Park.[83] Since it was the busy summer season, the campground was nearly full to capacity, with twenty-four of the twenty-seven campsites occupied. Some visitors

The entrance to the Soda Butte Campground in Montana's Gallatin National Forest, and just a few miles outside the northeastern entrance to Yellowstone National Forest.

Multiple Victims

were in hard-sided campers, while others were in tents.

The first attack occurred around 2 a.m. when a man sleeping in a tent awoke to feel the tent being moved, quickly followed by a bite to his leg. The man, Ronald Singer, punched the attacking bear through the tent fabric and the bear fled. Singer never saw the bear that attacked him.

While medical attention was being applied to Singer's wounds and lacerations, a scream rang out through the dark campground. The bear had approached another sleeping camper, biting Deborah Freele through the tent fabric, wounding her arm and leg. Freele screamed and then played dead. Other campers arrived in their vehicle, and once again the bear vanished into the night. She also never saw the bear that had attacked her only minutes after the Singer attack.

It would be several more hours, as the campground was being vacated, that officials would discover the body of Kevin Kammer at Campsite 26. The bear had attacked Kammer while he slept in his tent, pulling the victim out of the tent to a spot near the creek where the bear or bears had consumed a significant portion of his body.

Three separate attacks in one campground, all on campers sleeping in their tents, all within minutes of each other, and just a month after Erwin Evert's tragic death by another bear. It was unimaginable.

An intensive hunt for the guilty bears ensued, with the adult female grizzly captured within hours of the attacks, and her three yearlings captured within the next few days. The bears were moved to Bozeman, Montana as the investigation continued. The sow bear was euthanized, and her three yearlings transported to ZooMontana for permanent captivity. DNA testing of evidence revealed that the sow had been at the scene of all three attacks. While there was no DNA evidence linking the three yearlings to the three attacks, evidence indicated they had all fed on the third victim.

Although all four bears were in poor body condition, they were not outside the range to be expected of other wild bears in the ecosystem. Nutritional stress is not sufficient explanation for predatory bear behavior such as that exhibited by this female bear, investigators noted, concluding: "There is no clear explanation for the aggressive, predatory behavior of this adult female grizzly bear in the early morning hours of 28 July, 2010."

For the second consecutive year, a sow with four cubs of the year was documented in Yellowstone, with the ecosystem's grizzly population estimated to be at least 663 bears, and females with young were documented to inhabit all eighteen bear management units for the third year in a row.[84] Most of the 210 human-grizzly conflicts tallied during the year occurred outside the PCA, and most took place on private land in Wyoming. Yellowstone had a record high of 435 bear jams. Grand Teton saw an explosion in bear jams, as two related adult female grizzlies with their cubs of the year foraged alongside park roads. Some park bears ended up with their own Facebook pages and thousands of fans.

Grand Teton's roadside bears have their own human fan clubs, but there may be a biological basis for their existence since sow grizzlies with young cubs may select roadside habitats as a survival strategy for their offspring. Researchers in Scandinavia found that sow grizzlies with young cubs utilized less optimal habitat in order to avoid the risk of sharing better habitat with adult male bears that may kill cubs. Infanticide is common in grizzly bear populations, with most cubs killed by adult males during the mating season, bringing the sow bear back into estrus.[85]

Although sows with young cubs tend to restrict their movements, most may assume it's because of the limited mobility of the cubs. In reality, sows with young cubs may be elusive and sedentary as a strategy to enhance offspring survival, and especially to reduce the risk of infanticide. A study in Sweden found that sows that lost their cubs during the mating season moved more before their litter loss than females that kept their cubs throughout the mating season.[86]

The Scandinavian researchers also found that not only did sows with cubs avoid other adult grizzlies in order to protect their young, but changed their human-avoidance patterns. Instead of actively avoiding humans, some sows with cubs moved toward human settlements during the mating season—in essence using humans as shields against threats to their cubs by other bears. The study found that "successful mothers strongly selected for areas in relative close proximity to human habitation . . . whereas unsuccessful mothers avoided such areas." Successful sows moved their cubs into dense vegetation near human settlements, often without the humans being aware of their presence.[87]

Of the forty-eight known and probable grizzly bear deaths in the ecosystem in 2010, forty-three were human-caused, with fifteen hunting-related (including two mistaken identity by black bear hunters), and eleven self-defense kills. Five bears were removed due to human mortalities that year.

In early July, Yellowstone National Park officials removed a subadult male for his

A bear jam in Grand Teton National Park.

repeated nuisance activity, including bold behavior in a campground, and in September a subadult male was killed at a residence on the Wind River Indian Reservation in a self-defense action. Just two years prior, WG&F used remote cameras hung near blood lures to detect grizzly bear presence on the Wind River Indian Reservation, documenting the presence of an adult female with two yearling cubs, and a male, and three two-year-old bears, documenting continued grizzly bear range expansion.

In mid-October 2010, a hunter with an elk carcass was followed and approached by an adult female grizzly in the Crandall Creek area of the Shoshone National Forest. When the bear came in at very close range for a second time, the hunter killed her in self-defense.

A similar incident occurred with another bear less than a week later on the Bridger-Teton National Forest when a hunter first used pepper spray on a subadult male grizzly upon their first encounter in heavy timber, but the hunter shot and killed the bear when it returned a second time.

The small town of Clark, Wyoming had been in the headlines the year before when retired police officer Jerry Ruth was mauled by a sow grizzly near his home.[88] Just a year prior to the attack, Ruth had retired from the Baltimore County Police Department and had moved to Clark. Ruth and a buddy were walking through tall sagebrush to see if they could get a look at some elk when the sow came out of the brush and pounced on Ruth, biting his head. When the bear stopped the mauling and briefly moved away from him, Ruth looked up to see the bear had cubs. But when the bear turning back to him, Ruth pulled the revolver from his hip holster and fired three shots, killing the sow. Ruth survived his injuries, including a severely broken jaw and ribs. The three young cubs were live-captured and sent to the Memphis Zoo.[89]

In 2010, the town was back in the news. The subject was the town landfill, from which state officials had already removed two grizzlies. Although the landfill had previously attracted about a grizzly a year, the operation's dead animal pit was drawing a steady increase in predators, big and small. Landfill workers routinely carried bear spray and conducted a sweep of the area for bears before opening the gates to the public. Although bear advocates called for an electric fence to be constructed to deter bears, county officials held off while awaiting word from state environmental regulators who were in the process of assessing what rural landfills in the county may be closed in the future. It proved to be a good decision, since within a year, the open pit landfill would close, replaced by a system of large bins that were used to transport garbage from the area.

In late October, on Aldrich Creek in the Shoshone National Forest, a hunter (who received injuries) shot and killed an adult female grizzly in self-defense. There were nine incidents of grizzlies inflicting injuries on humans in 2010 within the Yellowstone ecosystem.

Return of the Grizzly

CHAPTER 10

DEADLY SUMMER

Yellowstone National Park officials closed a region of the park after grizzlies killed two people in 2011.

On the morning of July 6, 2011, Brian and Marylyn Matayoshi set out from the Wapiti Lake trailhead in the Canyon area of Yellowstone National Park, stopping about a mile down the trail to chat with another hiker as they photographed a sow grizzly and her two cubs about four hundred yards distant in an open valley away from the trail.[90] The Matayoshis resumed their hike, intending to walk a loop trail through the north end of Hayden Valley, but they encountered a swarm of mosquitos, forcing them to turn back. They soon came upon the same sow grizzly they had just photographed in the distance, but this time the bear was only one hundred yards away in a forested area just off the trail. When the Matayoshis saw the sow, they turned away, but the bear moved toward them. The couple then broke into a run down the trail, screaming as they fled the bear. The sow overtook Brian Matayoshi, quickly mauling and killing him while his wife hid behind some deadfall. The bear briefly walked over to Marylyn Matayoshi, picking her up by the backpack she had strapped on her back, and dropping her to the ground before leaving the scene. Other hikers heard the woman's screams for help and called 911. Rangers arrived within minutes.

The Wapiti sow grizzly involved in the attack was unmarked and had no known history of conflicts. Investigators determined that the bear's chase response was "most likely exacerbated" by the Matayoshis' yelling and running as they fled. The sow hit Brian Matayoshi hard, delivering a deadly blow to the head and biting his femoral artery, causing extensive blood loss. The Wapiti sow did not attempt to feed on the victims and fled the scene.

Investigators noted, "What possibility began as an attempt by the bear to assess the Matayoshis' activities became a sustained pursuit of them as they fled running and yelling on the trail." Determining that this attack resembled that of a surprise encounter rather than a predatory attack, the bear was not removed from the population. That would prove to be a fateful decision.

Early the morning of August 26, a father-daughter team out for a day-hike on the Mary Mountain Trail came upon human remains straddling the hiking trail, partially buried by dirt and debris.[91] John Wallace had been hiking alone on the day before when he was attacked and killed by a grizzly bear. The wounds on his arms indicate Wallace had tried to defend himself but was overcome by the bear. His partially consumed body was discovered just eight miles from the site of Brian Matayoshi's death just a few weeks earlier. DNA evidence at the scene indicated there were four bears at or near his body. Officials could not determine with certainty what

An audience gathers to watch grizzlies feed at the Grizzly and Wolf Discovery Center in West Yellowstone.

Return of the Grizzly

bear was responsible for killing Wallace, or why. But what they did learn was that the adult female grizzly and two cubs of the year that were involved in Matayoshi's death the month prior were likely involved in the consumption of Wallace's body. The Wapiti sow bear was euthanized and her cubs were removed from the population and relocated in West Yellowstone's Grizzly and Wolf Discovery Center, a permanent captive facility. Although the center is honest about the reasons why its animals come to be in captivity, most visitors are blissfully unaware that the beautiful bears named Grant and Roosevelt they watch behind fortified fences at the educational facility had once fed on humans.

The Yellowstone region's grizzly bear population had an annual growth rate between 4 and 7 percent from the 1980s through the 1990s, but by 2011, that rate had stabilized. In the prior few decades, areas outside the recovery zone were viewed more as population "sinks" for grizzlies, where the mortality rate exceeded the birth rate, but by 2011, population growth rates became more similar across the ecosystem, once again indicating the population had reached its carrying capacity.[92] But grizzlies remained under federal protections, and bear advocates were further fueled in arguments against delisting when research concluded that spawning cutthroat trout were no longer serving as an important food source for Yellowstone grizzlies, and that the loss of this food source resulted in grizzlies turning to elk calves as a primary food source.[93] For bear advocates, the loss of a major food source demonstrated the need for increased protections, and if grizzlies

Removed from Yellowstone National Park as a cub after feeding on a human, five-year-old Grant remains in captivity.

were turning to more meat eating, surely it would mean more trouble with livestock as bears would switch their food sources from declining elk populations to cattle and sheep.

With Yellowstone's grizzlies one of the most studied bear populations in the world, researchers have been able to document fascinating aspects of bear behavior, including a case of cub adoption in Grand Teton National Park. In July 2011, a five-year-old sow that already had two cubs of her own, adopted one of her fifteen-year-old mother's three cubs of the year. The two related sows shared an overlapping home range, were human-habituated, and were often seen along park roadsides. DNA analysis confirmed that the adopted cub was not with its birth mother. Bear managers noted that park visitors reported hearing sounds of intense bear fighting in the area frequented by both bears prior to the cub switching families.

This wasn't the first case involving cub adoption. Before 2007, adoption of cubs by grizzlies hadn't been documented in Yellowstone since the open pit garbage dump days of the late 1960s. The case involved two female grizzlies—one a well-known female at least twenty years old (Bear 125) with three young cubs, and the second female with her own two young cubs.[94] By mid-August 2007, the second (younger) female grizzly was seen with four cubs, while the older sow had only one. Although the reason for the adoption remains unknown, it is believed that the older sow had a confrontation with wolves, and was separated from two of her cubs at that time. Later research revealed that the two adult sows involved in this cub adoption were actually mother and daughter. Using bear hair retrieved from a hair collection site, park staff learned that

DNA from the hair samples indicated that the two cubs the younger sow had adopted were her full siblings; this meant their sire was the same adult male, an older male known as Scarface. So the younger sow raised her own two cubs (sired by another male bear, Bear 516), as well as her two siblings from a different litter. When the younger sow was located the next year, she was accompanied by only one yearling, indicating she had lost the other three cubs at some unknown time.

The year 2011 had one of the highest numbers of grizzly-human conflicts on record, with 229 incidents recorded, including fourteen cases of people injured or killed in conflicts with grizzlies. The two human mortalities had occurred in Yellowstone National Park, but as usual, most conflicts occurred outside the recovery zone, and over half the conflicts were on private property, mostly in Wyoming.

Of the thirty-seven human-caused grizzly deaths in 2011, eleven were hunting related, including one mistaken identity kill by a black bear hunter, and nine cases of self-defense including one that involved the capture and removal of an adult male grizzly that injured a hunter while defending a carcass in a state park in Wyoming in November. Bear managers also killed an adult female grizzly in November after the bear obtained multiple food rewards within the town of Dubois, Wyoming. Five people were injured by grizzly bears in Wyoming in 2011: four while hunting and one while hiking.[95]

Wyoming bear managers killed an adult male grizzly in the Grass Creek area near Worland after the bear broke into a house in early May. A sow and her two cubs of the year were removed from the South Fork of the Shoshone River area near Cody for nuisance activities resulting in food rewards at a private residence. In September, an archery hunter killed an adult female grizzly in self-defense. The sow's three cubs were considered probable bear deaths because of their age, so were included in the human-caused dead-bear count.

YNP managers killed a subadult male in early August after the bear was involved in numerous nuisance situations and had esca-

lating aggressive behavior towards humans. YNP recorded 414 bear jams, while Grand Teton National Park recorded 204.

By the end of the year, it was apparent that both female mortality and total mortality limits had been exceeded for 2011. Despite these thresholds being exceeded, bear managers throughout the ecosystem continued to document grizzly bear range expansion and breeding in new areas.

Cub adoption was documented in both Yellowstone and Grand Teton National Parks.

Deadly Summer

CHAPTER 11

REMOVING PROBLEM BEARS

A boar grizzly bear awaits his fate in a trap.

Attracted by the foul-smelling carcass of the calf he'd killed the day before, the grizzly bear climbed into the green metal box to resume feeding. As he grabbed the carcass with one huge front paw, the metal door of the cage slammed shut behind him. Trapped, the bear sprawled atop the carcass to wait out the night, knowing the human would arrive at first light. This bear had been trapped before.

WG&F bear specialist Zach Turnbull arrived on the scene at Wagon Creek in the Upper Green at dawn, finding the bear in the trap that he'd prepared the day before. Turnbull hooked the wheeled trap onto the hitch of his state-issued four-wheel drive pickup truck, and began his trip over rough roads in the Union Pass area of the Bridger-Teton National Forest. He would take the bear to an agency cabin where it could be processed and its future determined through consultation with others involved in managing this species once again listed as threatened pursuant to the federal Endangered Species Act.

But as Turnbull started down a gentle slope of the road, he touched his boot to the brakes, only to have the foot pedal fall to the floorboard with little resistance. Realizing the truck had lost its brakes, Turnbull managed to get the vehicle stopped and crawled underneath with tools to try to resolve the problem. Any direction of travel from here would involve mountain roads, curves, and switchbacks. The prior few days on the mountain had been rough ones for Turnbull, and this wasn't a stellar start for the new day.

As Turnbull worked on the truck, his aerosol can of bear pepper spray on the ground nearby, the big male grizzly bear intently observed him from the trap. The trapped bear was the sixth Upper Green grizzly bear Turnbull had handled in the last month after repeated depredations on cattle. Four others had been relocated out of the area in hopes they wouldn't prey on livestock again.

The bear stayed back in the shadows of his cage, a low growl rumbling from his chest when Turnbull moved around or approached too closely. At one point Turnbull walked near the back of the trap and the bear lunged at him, hitting the door to the trap and rocking the entire contraption, but Turnbull showed no visible response. He considered this bear's behavior to be fairly docile, considering its circumstances.

After about twenty minutes, another bear handler, Zach Gregory, a seasonal employee working with Turnbull, arrived. A temporary fix was made to the brakes, and the trap was transferred over to Gregory's truck and the men were ready to roll, headed to the Fish Creek Guard Station to begin their work.

WG&F's Zach Turnbull applies repairs to his agency vehicle, as a grizzly watches from a trap.

WG&F technician Zack Gregory prepares the bear's tranquilizer.

Removing Problem Bears

Turnbull climbs into the trap to examine the sleeping boar for identification marks.

a well-used notebook containing all the tag numbers, tattoo marks, and other identifying information about every known grizzly bear in the entire Yellowstone ecosystem. This was bear number 304, an old bear.

First captured in 1998 as a three-year-old, Bear 304 had been trapped and handled by wildlife officials on numerous occasions throughout his life, and had sported three different radio collars throughout his seventeen years roaming the ecosystem, but

Turnbull looks up the bear's information, learning that the bear was involved in numerous livestock depredations.

While Turnbull provided a distraction for the bear at the front of the trap, Gregory used a poke-stick to give the bruin a shot of tranquilizer in its meaty rear end. Within minutes, the bear began licking its lips and drooping, as the effects of the 1,500mg TELAZOL injection spread through its body. The bear soon slumped over the calf carcass in slumber.

Opening the trap door, the men made sure the bear was soundly sleeping before climbing in, straddling the bear to read the ear tag that had been placed in its right ear some years before: 1161. Turnbull climbed out of the trap to look the number up in

Return of the Grizzly

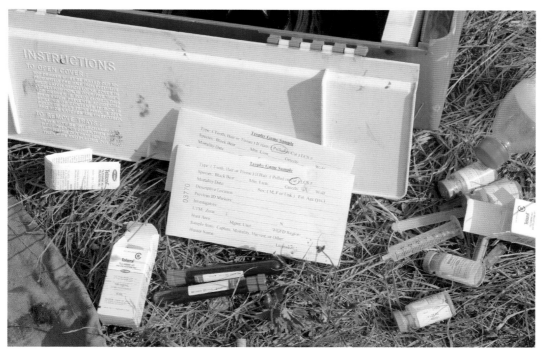

Collecting and recording biological samples from the boar grizzly.

was no longer wearing a collar. His rap sheet also noted that the bear had been captured and relocated in 2006 after preying on cattle. Ah, so this was not a first offense.

After calling in the bear's information to his agency managers, Turnbull climbed back into the trap to have a closer look at the bruin. The men had started to pull the bear out of the trap, but soon realized that his estimated 350-pound weight might mean that the men would be unable to lift him back into the trap if needed, so they would just have to do their work from inside the trap, straddling the latent beast.

The adult male grizzly was battle-scarred, with an open bloody gash on the right side of his head, just above the eye. "He took a whipping," Turnbull muttered, as his fingers probed the swollen mass near the eye, suggesting the bear may have a broken facial orb from a recent fight with another bear.

A look inside Bear 304's mouth revealed stained and worn teeth. One of his front paws had several broken claws and was entirely missing a fifth claw. A quick look at a hind foot showed it measured five and a half inches across. Turnbull's hands moved over the bear with the confidence and familiarity of one who has handled a lot of bears, and he repeatedly checked the bear's respiration, with quick taps on the bruin's nose to be sure the slumber was a deep one.

Turnbull and Gregory drew blood and hair samples from the bear while awaiting word of his fate. When the call came on the radio, it was no surprise that the bear would be destroyed instead of relocated. The decision to relocate or remove a bear is made after considering a number of

Removing Problem Bears

The battle-scarred old boar.

variables including age and sex of the bear, behavioral traits, health status, physical injuries or abnormalities, type of conflict, severity of conflict, known history of the bear, human safety concerns, and population management objectives. Turnbull quietly and professionally gave the bear a lethal injection as it continued to sleep from its earlier tranquilizer.

Turnbull climbed out of the trap as the bear's last breath escaped its body, acknowledging as he did so the sadness of having to kill such an animal. But the bear had lived a long life and had probably done his share of contributing to the gene pool many times over. Wounds such as those he had suffered would take their toll on his aging body, and he could have died from those wounds, or those suffered in future battles, or starved in his winter den. Death in nature is never

pleasant and often involves suffering. Instead, this bear had feasted on fresh beef for his last meal, and his life exited his body under the respectful hands of a caring wildlife professional. Perhaps it was not such a bad ending after all.

By the time that Turnbull trapped Bear 304 in August 2002, the minimum population estimate for Yellowstone grizzlies stood at 650, and in fact was probably closer to one thousand, according to state wildlife officials. The grizzly bear population had expanded to the point it is fairly common to see grizzly bears in this Upper Green, and much was being done to reduce the severity and frequency of depredations on livestock. Cattle producers and agency personnel intensively monitor the allotments for large carnivore conflicts, and wildlife agency personnel respond to confirmed depredations

Return of the Grizzly

by attempting to trap and remove the offending animals. Generally if it's a first-time offense, the bear can be relocated to another area not containing livestock, but if it's a repeat offender, the animal may be killed, effectively removing it from the population entirely. Of the six grizzlies trapped in the Upper Green River region in 2012, four were relocated while two others were destroyed.

FWS and its interagency cooperators continued to maintain that the Yellowstone grizzly bear population represents a viable population that is no longer in need of federal protections. The prompt removal of problem bears is believed to generate support for grizzly bear presence in local communities that co-inhabit these regions. Eliminating problem animals also helps reduce the likelihood that undesirable behaviors will be passed on or learned from bear-to-bear.

Turnbull and Gregory loaded the dead bear's carcass into the back of Gregory's pickup truck so it could be transported to a WG&F office. Bear 304's body would be handled by a taxidermist, and given to an educational institution as a tool to educate people about grizzly bears and their ecology. Bear 304's impact on the ecosystem would be felt for years to come.

Yellowstone National Park recorded nearly 4.5 million visitors in 2012, yet had few human-grizzly conflicts and no attacks on humans in the park that year, despite somewhat poor food conditions during spring and summer.

A bumper sticker on a Wyoming Game and Fish Department truck.

Additionally, spring carcass availability was the lowest on record—in the wake of wolf reintroduction and increased competition for carcasses. Yellowstone Lake cutthroat trout had been decimated to only ten percent of what it had been in year's past, and there was no evidence Yellowstone grizzlies were using what had once been an important food source. Bear use at moth sites was up 5 percent from the previous year, and whitebark pine cone production was good that fall. Research on the Bridger-Teton National Forest revealed that although tree stands that were heavily impacted by mountain pine beetle infestations saw reduced use by grizzlies, these radio-collared sows turned to ungulate carcasses during hunting season to meet their food needs. The 2012 bear research report noted, "It seems that hunter-killed elk and deer provided an alternative food source during fall in these areas with high whitebark pine mortality."[96]

There were fifty-five grizzly bear mortalities in the Yellowstone ecosystem in 2012, thirty-four of which were human-caused. Thirteen deaths were hunting related, with two of these being mistaken identity kills by black bear hunters, and the remaining eleven were self-defense kills. Five cubs of the year were assumed to be dead because their mothers were killed in these incidents. Another sixteen kills were due to management removals because of livestock depredations and site conflicts. Nine of the grizzly bear mortalities occurred outside the proposed demographic monitoring area. In September, several grizzlies were removed from private property in the North Piney Creek drainage west of Big Piney—in the Wyoming Range.

There were numerous cases of bears killing other bears in Yellowstone Park in

2012, such as when two adult sows were killed and consumed by other grizzly bears in May. One sow's two young cubs were assumed to have died as well, as well as two of the three cubs belonging to the other female. Wolves killed the third cub. Bear managers generally view bear-on-bear killings as further evidence that a population has reached its carrying capacity, but in these instances bear advocates pointed to these conflicts, as well as the decline in certain foods, as indicators that the bear population was food-stressed and required increased protections, not less.

Grand Teton National Park was the stage for further human-grizzly conflicts in 2012. In late November, a group of elk hunters in the park shot and killed a charging adult male grizzly in self-defense (at a distance of just ten feet), and the ensuing investigation revealed the bear had cached a cow elk carcass about fifty feet away. A special elk hunting season is allowed in Grand Teton National Park as part of its "elk reduction" program. This was the first hunter-killed grizzly bear in the history of the elk hunt, but a half-dozen people had been attacked or mauled by grizzlies in the park from 1994 to 2011. The park patrolled near three hundred bear jams (about as many as Yellowstone National Park that year), and utilized a "Wildlife Brigade" of paid and volunteer staff to educate the public about safe bear viewing. Bear advocates, appalled that a grizzly had been killed in a national park, called for an end to elk hunting in the park. Two Jackson Hole-based wildlife photographers and board members of the environmental group Wyoming Wildlife Advocates, and represented by a Washington, DC-based legal firm specializing in animal advocacy cases, filed a lawsuit in federal court in the nation's capital

challenging the legal authority of the elk hunts.

Both Grand Teton and Yellowstone ramped up their public education efforts, and installed bear-proof food storage boxes in area campgrounds. The small town of Clark, east of Yellowstone Park, discussed the need to reduce bear attractants in and around the town, as more grizzlies had been seen in the area, with state wildlife officials discussing the need for bear-proof garbage bins with local county commissioners.

Across Wyoming's border in eastern Idaho, bear managers responded to a few dozen human-grizzly conflicts, with most incidents involving bears frequenting developed area such as subdivisions or landfills, or killing livestock. During the fall archery hunt season for elk, two hunters surprised a grizzly bear on its day bed while they were tracking a wounded elk, and one of the hunters was injured by the bear in the encounter. Idaho bear managers noted that with the increase in bear numbers and distribution in Idaho, the increasing trend on the number of conflicts was to be expected.

In Montana's portion of the Yellowstone ecosystem, state officials investigated forty-six grizzly-human conflicts, with most conflicts occurring on private property and over a larger geographic area as the grizzly population expanded. Most conflicts involved bears in developed areas, or bears involved in livestock depredations, but there were two cases involving human injury. Both cases involved surprise encounters with female bears with young cubs, and one involved an archery hunter, while the other was a mountain biker.

Wyoming recorded 213 grizzly-human conflicts, including 130 cases of livestock depredations, twenty-nine cases of property damage, and twenty-four cases of bears in garbage. In addition, there were three cases of human injuries inflicted by grizzlies (two hunters were injured, and one person was injured while sleeping on the ground), and five other cases involving grizzly bear aggression towards humans. Most conflicts occurred in the areas of Teton County adjacent to Grand Teton National Park, as well as the Upper Green of Sublette County.

The increasing trend in conflicts in Wyoming was accounted for by the increase in numbers and distribution of grizzlies into areas used by humans on both public and private land. Wyoming bear managers noted "there is less social and biological suitability for bear occupancy in areas further from the recovery zone due to development, land use patterns, and various forms of recreation."

Wyoming recorded three cases of human injuries due to conflicts with grizzlies, as well as five other cases of grizzlies behaving aggressively towards humans but not causing injury in 2012.[97]

In a keynote address at an international human-bear conflicts workshop in 2012, FWS's Chris Servheen said that bear managers were somewhat victims of their own success—that bears are now in places where they were never expected to be ten or twenty years prior. Grizzly bear range expansion in the Yellowstone ecosystem had increased 38 percent from 2004 to 2010, with most expansion occurring in the northern and southern regions of the ecosystem.

In just a few years, grizzlies expanded their range nearly 40 percent.

Removing Problem Bears

CHAPTER 12

BIZARRE ENCOUNTERS

The generally increasing trend of human-grizzly conflicts continued in 2013, including two bear attacks in one day, leaving four people with minor injuries.

If any one year's human-grizzly conflicts could be summarized as bizarre, 2013 would be a contender for the title, with incidents ranging from four people receiving minor injuries all in the same day in two separate grizzly bear attacks, to severe attacks resulting from random encounters between grizzlies and humans.

A man irrigating his fields early one June morning was attacked and mauled by a grizzly after his dog surprised a sow grizzly bear and her cubs on private property in the South Fork area west of Cody. The man attempted to defend himself with his shovel, but received extensive injuries to his face, head, back, legs, and arms. The man, a former board member of the Greater Yellowstone Coalition, asked that the bear's life be spared. Although WG&F officials initially set traps in the area of the attack, they suspended the effort after tracking the sow and cubs as the animals

Yellowstone National Park reported that a sow grizzly with a cub injured two people in a surprise encounter.

moved into a more remote location away from homes.

Two separate grizzly bear attacks on one August day left four people with minor injuries. The first incident occurred on a trail in Yellowstone National Park. Four hikers encountered a grizzly cub on the trail shortly before the cub's mother charged the group, injuring two of the hikers as two of the four deployed their pepper spray. A second incident occurred just a half-hour later near Island Park, Idaho, when two researchers startled a grizzly on its day bed. The bear charged and bit one man on the leg as she knocked him down. When his research partner attempted to spray the bear with pepper spray, the sow bit the man's hands before running away.

Idaho tallied twenty-four bear-human conflicts that year, including another incident involving human injury near Island

Park in which a third researcher surprised a grizzly at close range and was bitten on the arm before the bear fled. DNA tests later revealed that the two grizzlies involved in the two attacks on researchers that summer had both had previous run-ins with humans and bit people before fleeing.

In September, a bowhunter pursuing elk in the Bridger-Teton National Forest was attacked during a surprise encounter with an adult grizzly. The man broke his leg and suffered puncture wounds on his back before his hunting companions managed to scare the bear away.[98]

Wyoming's generally increasing trend of grizzly-human conflicts continued, including 152 recorded incidents in 2013. There were five cases of grizzly bear aggression towards humans recorded, and two grizzlies were killed in self-defense encounters.

Some attacks resulted from surprise encounters with grizzlies on their daybeds, but in these cases, injuries are usually minor.

WG&F met their goal of maintaining radio collars on twenty-five female grizzly bears in the state's portion of the ecosystem (outside the national parks) through the agency's capture efforts in 2013.[99] During the last two weeks of May, eight grizzlies were captured in the Dubois area (including one bear that was captured twice) and collars were placed on five. Trapping efforts then moved to the Upper Green for most of the month of July, with three grizzlies captured during the effort, and radio transmitters placed on all three. Apparently the capture effort wasn't too traumatic for the bears since one of the bears was captured a total of nine times. WG&F aerial over-flights documented at least 241 grizzlies located outside Yellowstone National Park's borders in western Wyoming.

Most of the 152 human-grizzly conflicts in Wyoming in 2013 involved livestock depredations or grizzlies seeking out foods associated with humans (beehives, garbage, pet or livestock feed. Ninety-two percent of conflicts occurred outside the Primary Conservation Area (recovery zone) as the grizzly bear population continued to expand its range. Southwestern Montana was then having a similar experience, with a 28 percent increase in conflict numbers over the past decade.

There were twenty-three human-caused grizzly deaths in the Yellowstone ecosystem in 2013, including ten management removals due to livestock depredations or site conflicts, and seven self-defense killings of grizzlies.

Food availability in Yellowstone Park was poor in spring, but improved later in the

Return of the Grizzly

The greatest source of human-caused grizzly bear mortality in the Yellowstone ecosystem was self-defense killings.

year. The park had few human-grizzly conflicts in 2013, but that number did include an attack on two people by sow grizzly with a young cub in a surprise encounter in an area with poor visibility. Park officials worked to record bear behavior during encounters with humans in the park, finding that grizzly bears rarely reacted aggressively during these encounters, and most bears remained neutral or moved away. The National Park Service ramped up its public bear-safety education campaign, installed more bear-proof food storage boxes, and hazed grizzlies away from developed areas, roadsides, and campgrounds more than seventy-five times. The park tallied 331 roadside bear jams as people congregated to watch habituated bears.

The year 2013 was a peak year for documentation of sows with cubs of the year in the ecosystem, with an all-time high of fifty-eight tallied. As the year drew to close, the IGBST released its completed report on changes to food resources for the Yellowstone region's grizzlies, a concerted attempt to address the issues the federal court had identified when it ruled grizzlies must remain under federal protection. In short, the fifty-eight-page document demonstrated the Yellowstone grizzly bear's ability to successfully shift major food items in their diet as availability changes, and that a recent decline in cub survival was an indication of grizzly bear density rather than a lack of available resources.

The paper concluded:

Grizzly bears obtained sufficient alternative foods through diet shifts and have maintained body mass and percent body fat over time. Based on extensive demographic analyses completed to date, we have not observed a decline in the Yellowstone grizzly bear population but only a slowing of population growth since the early 2000s, possibly indicating the population is near carrying capacity. Evidence from demographic analyses indicates that the change in population trajectory was more associated with grizzly bear density, primarily through reduced cub survival and reproductive transition, rather than whitebark pine decline.[100]

Bear advocates contested the paper and its findings as politically motivated, designed to provide a basis for removing grizzlies from federal protection.

Prior to 2013, population parameters such as sows with young were only counted for grizzlies that occurred within the official

Greater Yellowstone Ecosystem Grizzly Bear Population

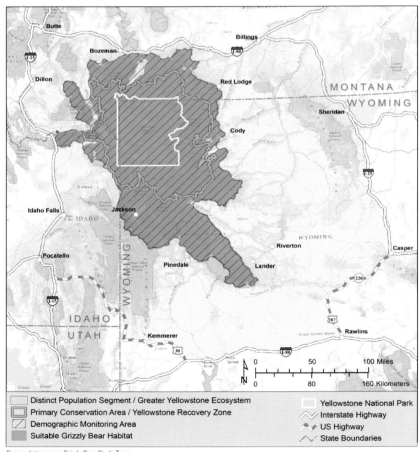

Source: Interagency Grizzly Bear Study Team

Return of the Grizzly

recovery zone/conservation management area—no matter how many grizzlies occurred outside this zone. But bear managers changed the monitoring protocol in 2013 in order to incorporate grizzlies that occur within the area defined as suitable grizzly habitat, the Demographic Monitoring Area (DMA). Even with the much larger monitoring zone, grizzly sows with cubs outside this zone are not counted toward population monitoring protocols. In 2014, there were three sows with young confirmed outside the DMA. Six bear mortalities, all adult males, were recorded outside the DMA, and four adult sows with cubs were also discovered outside this much larger DMA. As federal officials continued to expand the monitoring area for grizzlies, the bear population continued to step outside that zone.

The 2014 report of the Interagency Grizzly Bear Study Team noted that the Yellowstone region's grizzly bear population had begun recovery in the mid-1980s, with robust population growth during the 1990s, followed by a slowing of population growth in conjunction with a decline in cub and yearling survival rates. Although much attention was focused on whether this was due to changes in food availability (such as spawning cutthroat trout, whitebark pine cone production, ungulate carcasses, and insect aggregations), the team reported once again that "increased grizzly bear density, rather than a decline in food resources, may be a driver of this change in population trajectory, possibly indicating the population is nearing carrying capacity."[101]

From the 1950s through the 1970s, most grizzly bear mortalities in Yellowstone National Park had been due to human causes, but in recent decades, most mortalities were from natural causes, intraspecific strife (bears killing bears) and predation.

Winter-killed ungulate carcasses were more abundant in Yellowstone National Park in 2014 than they had been for the previous two years, and whitebark pine cone production was up as well. There were nineteen human-caused grizzly mortalities in the Yellowstone ecosystem in 2014, with nine grizzlies removed from the population due to repeated livestock depredations, nine hunting-related (including seven bears killed in self-defense), and one adult male bear that was maliciously killed (shot and left) in Montana's Gallatin National Forest.

It was also a relatively quiet year in terms of human-bear conflicts—at least until that fall when a man was killed in a national forest in Wyoming. But most conflicts were minor: in Yellowstone, a grizzly ripped the siding off a backcountry patrol cabin to get to a mouse nest between the walls; a grizzly tore up empty ice cream buckets that had been cleaned and left on the loading dock at a park convenience store; and in two cases, bears damaged property (including a tent in a campground) and obtained food rewards in the process. Yellowstone park officials documented 351 bear jams in 2014.

Montana's situation was a little different, with forty-one conflicts in Montana's portion of the ecosystem, including three people who sustained injuries in two conflicts with grizzlies (two people sustained minor injuries while being knocked down by a grizzly, and a black bear hunter was severely mauled by an adult male grizzly) and two cases of grizzly bears killed in self-defense. Private property near Red Lodge—which had no cases of livestock depredations by grizzlies just five years prior—now racked up depredation events every year as the grizzly population expanded north out of Wyoming.

Most (130) of the 164 grizzly-human conflicts in Wyoming involved livestock

A subadult male grizzly from one of Grand Teton National Park's famous roadside sows was killed after repeated livestock depredations in 2014.

depredations, but there was one human mortality, two other cases of human injury, and four cases of grizzly bear aggression toward humans. The Wind River Reservation also recorded two cases of grizzly aggression, including a person that was chased on foot by a grizzly, and two people on an all-terrain vehicle that were chased by a sow grizzly with cubs.

The subadult male cub of Grand Teton's roadside Sow 399 was killed after repeated livestock depredations in 2014. Although the bear spent his first few years within the confines of the park, he moved on after that, and after hanging out in a residential subdivision, had been relocated into the northern portion of the park. In following years, the bear killed numerous cattle and sheep over a two-year period in the Upper Green and was relocated back to Grand

Teton again, but he returned to the Upper Green in 2014. After a killing spree involving the death of nine or ten cattle within a few days, the bear was finally destroyed by bear managers.

Frank Craighead had described how bears congregated on the garbage dumps in Yellowstone National Park: "Over the years they came in ever-increasing numbers from farther and farther away, until the early summer influx became an annual migration."[102] Just as grizzlies congregate around other food sources—be it salmon spawning runs, logging or mineral exploration camps, garbage dumps, or insect aggregations—grizzlies in the Upper Green exhibited the same behavior, congregating as the cattle entered the allotment. Sublette County cattle had become a regional eco-center for the region's grizzlies.

Return of the Grizzly

As the grizzly bear population expanded into new areas, conflicts escalated.

In 2014, sixteen grizzlies were relocated in Wyoming (most for killing cattle in the Upper Green) and six grizzlies were removed from the population (three for livestock depredations, and three due to property damage or human food rewards and "exhibiting unnaturally bold behavior in close proximity to humans").[103] There were 164 recorded grizzly-human conflicts in Wyoming that year, with 140 of the conflicts involving livestock. There was one human death, two cases of human injury, and seven other incidents involving grizzlies exhibiting aggression towards humans.

Adam Stewart set out from the Brooks Lake Trailhead of the Bridger-Teton National Forest mid-morning on Thursday, September 4, 2014, hiking up the Cub Creek Trail into the Teton Wilderness. It was a beauti-

ful day for a hike, sunny and cool, with light winds. An experienced backcountry hiker, thirty-one-year-old Stewart was working for a private company under contract with the US Forest Service to survey vegetation plots. Five miles down the trail, Stewart found a spot for his overnight camp, setting up his tent, and hanging his food supply out of reach of any neighborhood bears.[104]

It was early afternoon when Stewart set off on another hike, headed toward the survey plot three miles distant. According to the time stamp of the image captured by his camera, Stewart stopped at 2:33 p.m. to admire the rugged beauty of the jagged cliff face of the mountains of the Continental Divide spread out south of Cub Creek. Stewart then crossed into an unnamed tributary to Cub Creek, following a game trail that took him through tall stands of timber, and then hiking up over a rise in the undulating landscape. That rise is the location investigators believe Stewart encountered the bear or bears that killed him—only minutes after he took the photograph of the wild countryside in which he worked. Stewart's remains were found eight days later, scattered in a food cache typical of a bear, mixed in with the remains of a mule deer carcass, and covered with a few inches of snow from the storm that settled over the area during the interagency search for the missing man. Stewart had been killed by blunt force injuries to his skull from a bear bite, and his remains had been almost completely consumed.

Investigators found that a bear or bears had cached not only Stewart's remains, but that of two mule deer. Hair samples collected within a half-mile radius of the remains were used to identify three grizzly bears (one female and two males) as well as one male black bear. Hair samples at the fatality site itself were from both an adult male grizzly bear and an adult male black bear. None of the bears were known bears in the Yellowstone ecosystem—meaning that none of the bears had been previously identified or captured by wildlife managers in the past. But it was impossible to determine which, if any, of the bears documented at the site were directly responsible for Stewart's death. According to the Board of Review Report on Stewart's death, investigators believe that the fatal attack was the result of a combination of "an encounter with a bear on a food source; and/or a surprise encounter with a bear due to the poor visual sight distance. Given the evidence, it is likely that a combination of these factors was the cause of Mr. Stewart's encounter with a bear that resulted in his death."

With the presence of so many bears near the fatality site, and the duration of time between when Stewart was killed and when his remains were recovered, there was no way to definitely determine what bear killed him, although officials contend it was most likely a grizzly. Hair found on the victim's clothing was determined to be "most probably grizzly bear" according to the forensic laboratory examination report.

Fatal grizzly bear attacks are rare, but attacks by grizzlies in the Yellowstone region are increasing.

After Adam Stewart's death, the Board of Review developed a set of recommendations for all private or government organizations working in bear country to follow, including:

- provide bear safety training;
- structure work parties to include groups of at least two people, or from horseback;
- encourage employees to carry bear spray;
- require workers to provide trip itineraries; and implement standard practice for worker check-in when returning from the backcountry to enable faster rescue or recovery.[105]

A few weeks after Adam Stewart's death, a sow grizzly with cubs attacked and injured a bowhunter not far from where Stewart's body had been found, although state officials said there was no evidence linking the incidents. Two well-camouflaged hunters were hiding as they scoped for elk, when the sow saw movement and immediately charged. The sow bit one hunter, while the other sprayed the grizzly with pepper spray before she fled the scene. The wounded hunter suffered only minor injuries.

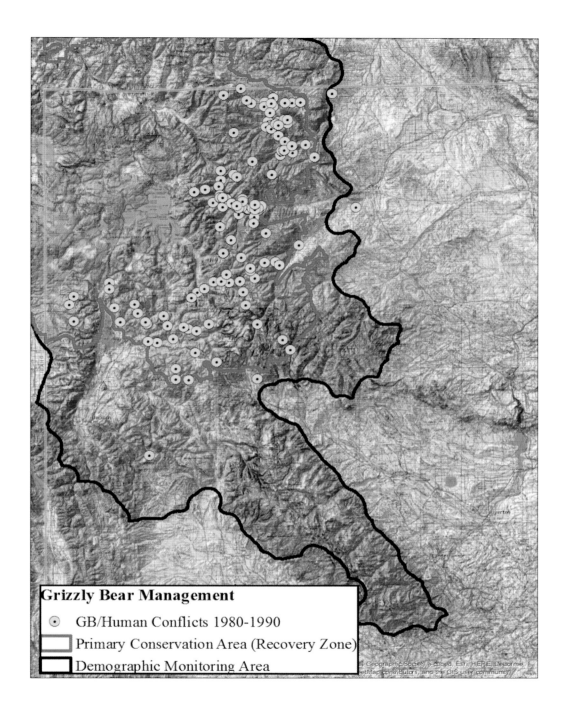

Grizzly Bear Management

⊙ GB/Human Conflicts 1980-1990

☐ Primary Conservation Area (Recovery Zone)

☐ Demographic Monitoring Area

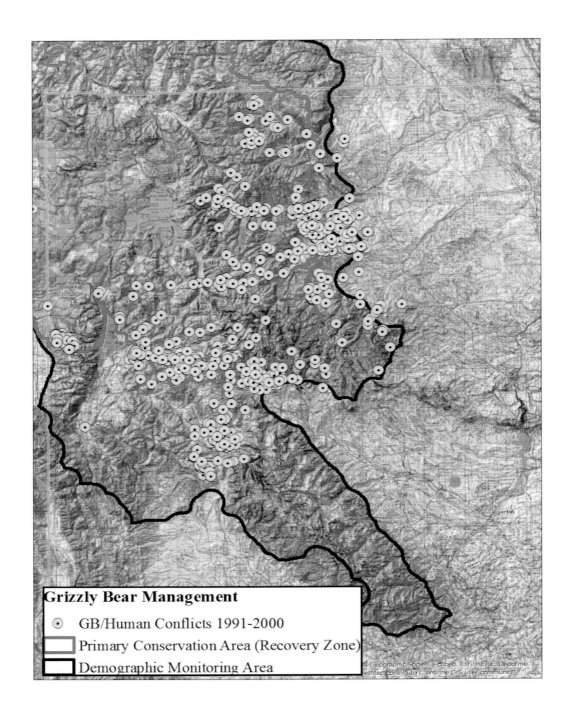

Grizzly Bear Management

⊙ GB/Human Conflicts 1991-2000

☐ Primary Conservation Area (Recovery Zone)

☐ Demographic Monitoring Area

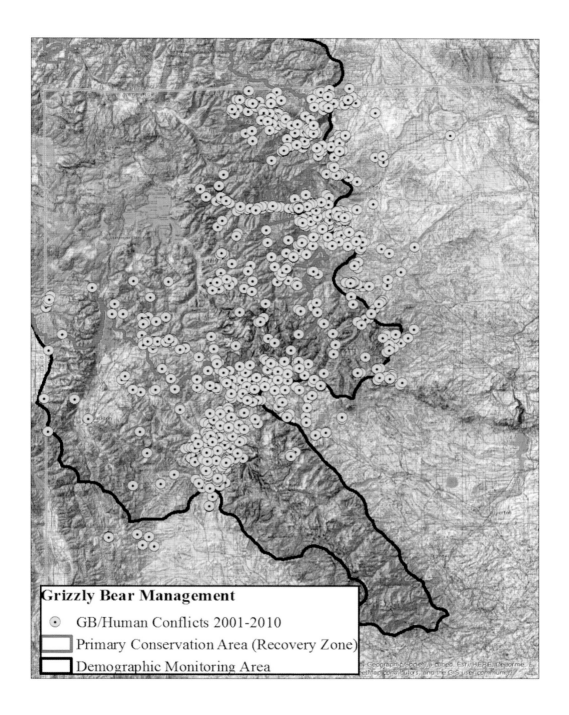

Grizzly Bear Management

- ⊙ GB/Human Conflicts 2001-2010
- ☐ Primary Conservation Area (Recovery Zone)
- ☐ Demographic Monitoring Area

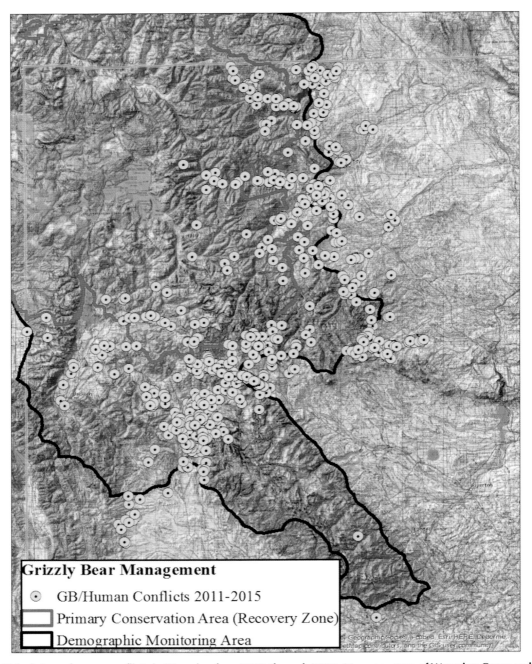

Grizzly bear–human conflicts in Wyoming from 1980 through 2015. Maps courtesy of Wyoming Game and Fish Department.

Return of the Grizzly

CHAPTER 13

THE PROBLEM WITH HABITUATION

A boar grizzly bear crosses between lines of photographers in Grand Teton National Park.

Yellowstone and Grand Teton National Parks have become go-to destinations for visitors to view bears roaming the roadsides while rangers strictly control bear jams of people and traffic. But what happens when human-habituated bears cross outside the park's boundaries where there are no rangers, but towns and cities and rural residences? Often their human habituation leads to their demise.

Yellowstone celebrates its success at managing humans at bear jams. With strict provisions in place to ensure that bears are not receiving food rewards from humans, it's humans that are managed along park roadsides, rather than bears. The benefit of this policy is that bears can seek out natural foods in high-quality habitat along the park's roadsides and developments, avoiding possible conflicts in the social hierarchy of the higher-density bear population in the park's more remote locations. Instead of fleeing the scene each time they encounter a human, the bears become accustomed to

Photographers in Grand Teton National Park.

vehicles and the thousands of people that stop to view and photograph them—the process of habituation. The resulting human habituation is distinct from food conditioning, which poses a threat to human safety as the bears inevitably seek out food from humans. Park bear managers are careful to keep bears from becoming food conditioned, but maintain that habituation is not necessarily detrimental to bears or people. The plus side is the expectation of seeing grizzly bears along park roadsides increases visitation to the park, and generates millions of dollars in tourism revenue each year to the park's gateway communities.

According to park bear managers, "Key components of a successful habituated bear management program include preventing bears from becoming conditioned to human foods and garbage, making human activities as predictable as possible, and setting certain boundaries for both bears and people."[106]

But the park service tends to gloss over the fact that grizzlies that become human habituated in the safety of national parks sometimes leave the parks, entering areas where humans live year-round and where human-habituated bears aren't tolerated. Bears inhabiting Grand Teton National Park are particularly at risk, since the park is much smaller than Yellowstone and grizzly bears tend to roam large ranges. The unfortunate story of Bear 760 is a case in point.

In late October 2014, the Wyoming Game and Fish Department responded to a report of a grizzly bear outside a residence in Clark, Wyoming, some fifty miles east of Yellowstone. Returning from a deer hunt, the homeowner had hung his deer in a tree, only to find a grizzly bear had discovered

Return of the Grizzly

the carcass, and tore it down. When the man used his pickup truck to try to drive the bear away from the carcass, the grizzly bear refused to budge. WG&F arrived at the scene, waited for the bear to move off the carcass and set a leg snare near the remains of the deer. When the grizzly moved back to reclaim the carcass, he was captured and sedated with a tranquilizer. When the bear manager examined the bear, he found this was a known bear with a rap sheet: Bear 760. Following agency guidelines, and in consultation with FWS, WG&F administered a lethal injection to the bear because

A boar grizzly rubs against a utility pole in Grand Teton National Park. The pole is a popular rubbing spot for grizzlies.

of his conflict history, habituation, and close association to people and developed areas.

Bear 760 was a well-known grizzly. Born in 2011 in Grand Teton National Park, he had grown up sharing the roadside habitat with this famous roadside mother and grandmother, and had been photographed and viewed by thousands of adoring fans throughout his lifetime. His mother was the younger sow that had adopted one of her mother's cubs that same year. When Bear 760 reached the age of independence, he moved on his own through Grand Teton, and in September 2014, he took up temporary residence along the Moose-Wilson Road, drawing hundreds of photographers daily, creating bear jams, and eventually prompting the temporary closure of the road while he lingered. His roaming eventually took him beyond the park to a high-end residential subdivision outside of Jackson, comfortable among the houses, traffic, and people. Well-habituated to living life in the presence of humans, one day the grizzly approached at close range a man walking his dog in the subdivision, and continued to hang out in the area. Concerned for human safety, WG&F decided to relocate the habituated bear to a more remote area. On October 10, Bear 760 was released on 5-Mile Creek in the Shoshone National Forest about five miles east of Yellowstone. The male grizzly made his way from the mountains where he had been relocated, winding up in a residential yard in Clark, where he took a stand guarding the deer carcass he had procured.

Bear advocates were outraged that the bear had been destroyed, claiming that the bear's human habituation didn't justify its death. His grieving fans held a memorial service.

The Problem with Habituation

Less than an hour after the boar stopped for by for a rub, Sow 610 with her two yearlings investigated the scene.

Should Bear 760 have been killed to protect human safety? Bear advocates say no, that habituated bears view humans "as a benevolent part of their world" and state bear managers need to show more tolerance for these animals.[107] But bear managers knew that grizzly bears had killed two people, and mauled and wounded several others, within the last few years within sixty miles of the town of Clark.

A year after the death of Bear 760, in a special issue of *Yellowstone Science* focused on Yellowstone grizzly bear recovery, park officials acknowledged the problems that are sometimes caused by the habituation of bears that exist in the safety and control of the parks. It noted:

In national parks, where humans are temporary visitors and their activities and infrastructures are highly controlled, habituated bears have been managed in a manner to reduce human-bear conflicts, allow for popular recreational bear viewing, and maximize the effectiveness of available habitat. However, in areas outside of national parks where human activities are less strictly regulated, habituation can greatly increase the chances of bears becoming conditioned to human foods or being involved in other types of human-bear conflicts that put both humans and bears at significant risk. Tolerance and management of bear habituation to people may work for some land management agencies under highly controlled and predictable situ-

Return of the Grizzly

A yearling grizzly has a go at the same utility pole.

ations, such as national parks, where habituation would typically not be an appropriate bear behavior under less controlled situations with completely different contexts. Habituated bears are still wild bears and should not be considered otherwise. It is important for the public to understand that habituation is sometimes unavoidable, and impacts both wildlife and people; and the way habituation is addressed by wildlife managers is extremely site and situation specific.[108]

That humans merely are temporary visitors to national parks, which are areas where human activity is tightly controlled, is an often-neglected point. Grizzlies that leave the national parks enter the real world in which humans inhabit every day. Human lifestyles

have changed in response to increased grizzly bear presence outside the parks.

Farmers encounter grizzlies in their open corn and bean fields outside of Powell, miles from mountain habitats. Parents near Cody don't allow their children to play outside in their yards during warm summer months. Only after grizzlies have entered their winter dens can the children roam their own yards.

Campers in the Brooks Lake area near Dubois are no longer able to use soft-sided tents or sleep under the stars. Backcountry guides and guest ranch owners throughout the Bridger-Teton National Forest make sure that every camp is equipped with dogs to keep bears at bay, and ensure that guests who want to go for a walk on the Shoshone National Forest take one of the dogs with them.

The Problem with Habituation

Grizzly bear tracks on an irrigation pipeline in northwestern Wyoming. Photo courtesy Wyoming Game and Fish Department.

Backcountry skiers and photographers carry firearms or bear spray on their hips, as do sheep herders and cowboys—and are expected to do so, even when on their private property.

There are an average of nine grizzly bears killed outside the national parks in the Yellowstone region in self-defense every year. Let that register: Nine cases. Every year. In self-defense. Legal prosecution is rare, because self-defense is a justified cause for killing a grizzly in this region inhabited by up to one thousand of the great bruins. There were ninety-seven grizzlies killed in self-defense or defense of others in the Yellowstone ecosystem in the last decade, and as federal bear managers note: "self-defense

mortalities will always be a reality when conserving a species that is capable of killing humans."[109] Regardless, mortality rates were low enough to allow the grizzly bear population to increase in numbers and range.

This is the reality of what it's like to live with a recovered grizzly bear population. It's not just in rural areas. In 2015, grizzly bears were located in downtown Dubois, and just outside of the Thermopolis and Cody city limits.

After an interagency group of grizzly bear managers reviewed recent bear mortalities, the group issued a report recommending that bowhunters should have a hunting partner and their bear spray at the ready while calling for elk. The report noted, "They need to know that elk calling in the fall is very attractive to grizzlies and they are just as likely to get a grizzly to respond as they are to get an elk to respond."[110]

In total, 76 percent of all grizzly bear deaths in the Yellowstone ecosystem are, in one way or another, caused by humans. But as US Fish and Wildlife Service notes, "some mortality, including most human-caused mortality, is unavoidable in a dynamic system where hundreds of bears inhabit large areas of diverse habitat with several million human visitors and residents."[111]

Park officials report that in the last twenty-five years, there have been more than twelve thousand bear jams in Yellowstone, with not a single bear attack on a human, discrediting concerns that tolerating habituated bears would result in human injury.[112]

But habituated bears occurring outside the safety zone of the national parks would continue to be the subject of controversy.

WG&F's Zach Turnbull said, "You're looking at managing bears across three

Return of the Grizzly

Roadside grizzlies in Grand Teton National Park.

states, two national parks, and an Indian reservation, with different jurisdictions, different rules, locals and non-locals, whatever. You take highly human habituated bears and throw them out on that landscape and they have a much less probability to survive."

"If you're a bear advocate that's bad," he said. "If you're a human safety advocate, that's probably bad because they will probably get into conflicts with humans that causes that decreased rate of survivorship."

"We're managing roadside bears on state highways now that are not 40 mph zones with pullouts" like those in national parks, he said, pointing to this example: a car traversing 65 mph over Togwotee Pass (a winding mountain highway linking Jackson Hole with Dubois) stops in the middle of the road so the car occupants can enjoy

the human-habituated grizzly along the roadside. A semi-tractor-trailer hauling a load of hay comes over a hill and encounters the car stopped in the roadway. In this scenario, the mere presence of the human-habituated bear has created additional safety problems.

While Grand Teton National Park can close a road because of grizzly bear presence, or shut down an area to campers, Turnbull said, "we don't have the flexibility in the state." State officials can't kick a landowner off their land, or close a highway, and don't have the management authority offered by exclusive jurisdiction. "They have tools that they can use to mitigate some of those issues that we just can't."

While the park service has the option to move people away from a bear, through road and area closures, Turnbull said, "We don't have the option of taking the people off, and it's not realistic to think that we do."

In 2015, bear managers throughout the Yellowstone ecosystem were finding grizzlies in places the bears hadn't roamed for one hundred years, and black bear hunters were recording grizzlies coming to their bear baits near South Pass, Wyoming in the southern portion of the Wind River Range, and along the eastern front of the Wyoming Range west of Big Piney—not only far outside the grizzly recovery zone, but far outside what had been determined to be suitable grizzly habitat. An adult male grizzly was captured and relocated away from a private residence where he was killing domestic chickens and ducks southwest of Cody in September 2015; a sow with two yearling cubs was moved for eating apples and frequenting developed areas west of Cody the same month; and a sow with cubs was relocated from the Cody landfill in November.

In total, WG&F captured forty-five grizzly bears in an attempt to prevent or resolve conflicts in 2015, with most captures involving lone grizzly bears of all age classes.[113] Most of the captures took place in Park and Sublette counties, and about half were a result of bears killing livestock. Twelve management captures occurred as preemptive measures for bears exhibiting habituated behavior and/or being in close proximity to people, as well as three non-target captures and two captures for property damage. All relocated grizzly bears were released on US Forest Service lands in or adjacent to the recovery zone/primary conservation area.

Seventeen captures resulted in the removal of grizzly bears from the population by WG&F personnel by lethal removal or live placement in a zoo. These bears were removed due to a history of previous conflicts, a known history of close association with humans, or because they were deemed unsuitable for release into the wild; these animals included orphaned cubs, bears in poor physical condition, or those that posed a human safety concern.

Return of the Grizzly

CHAPTER 14

SHEEP STATION

A grizzly sow with fresh battle wounds on her head.

There are advocacy groups in the western United States that bill themselves as environmental organizations but whose primary purpose appears to be to rid the western rangelands of public lands for livestock grazing—an important and long-standing economic foundation for many western rural communities. Western Watersheds Project is one group that uses litigation against federal agencies in its attempt to destabilize the livestock industry; others include the Center for Biological Diversity and WildEarth Guardians. These groups use the power of the Endangered Species Act as a tool to bludgeon livestock producers, routinely suing federal agencies overseeing livestock grazing and making behind-closed-door settlement agreements that reduce or restricting grazing. The case of the US Sheep Experiment Station is a prime example.

In August 2012, wildlife officials found the radio-collar that had been cut off a male grizzly bear and hidden under a log in a stream on lands owned by US Sheep

Experiment Station that straddles the Idaho-Montana border west of Yellowstone National Park—in a pasture located outside the grizzly bear recovery zone. The bear's body was never found, but a hunter's camp was located nearby, and a domestic sheep flock had grazed the area under the full-time supervision of a sheepherder and a mixture of livestock guardian and herding dogs. The case remains unsolved. That would not stop anti-grazing groups from using this presumed grizzly bear death as reason to call for a prohibition of sheep grazing on the Sheep Station's own property, disregarding the fact that this pasture was located outside the bear recovery zone. By this time in the grizzly recovery process, all of the domestic sheep grazing allotments within the grizzly bear recovery zone had already been closed, but environmental groups soon began hounding that wherever grizzlies

occurred, domestic sheep grazing should be halted. At the same time, the grizzly bear had been delisted and then relisted again, and in 2010, the Sheep Station agreed not to use two of its allotments (the Meyers Creek Forest Service allotment within the recovery zone, which was only used for trailing sheep, and the East Range allotment located entirely on Sheep Station lands outside the recovery zone and used for summer grazing but accessed only through the Meyers Creek allotment) until a full environmental impact statement on its grazing program could be completed. It appeared that this was a temporary closure, agreed to in order to mollify the activists.

The Sheep Station had been established by the Woodrow Wilson administration in 1918, and was now managed by the USDA Agricultural Research Service (ARS) as a center for agricultural research focused on

Domestic sheep in US Sheep Experiment Station pens.

Return of the Grizzly

range sheep production. Among its decades of research projects—ranging from the use of livestock guardian dogs, studying infectious diseases, to grazing management and improving genetic traits to enhance lamb production—the Sheep Station is credited with the development of three popular domestic sheep breeds: the Columbia, Targhee, and Polypay. The station is well known in the national livestock industry for its efforts to manage domestic sheep grazing on sagebrush steppe to preserve native ecosystems. The flock that grazes the Sheep Station is owned by its research partner, the University of Idaho, and managed in a series of allotments that straddled the Idaho-Montana border. The Sheep Station holds an exclusive title to some of its grazing land, but it also holds leases to graze lands administered by the Department of Energy, National Forest, and Bureau of Land Management.

The year before the grizzly bear's radio-collar was found on Sheep Station property, the US Fish and Wildlife Service (FWS) examined the impacts of the Sheep Station's overall grazing program and had determined that while some "take" of grizzly bears could be expected because of anticipated conflicts, continued grazing "will not appreciably reduce the likelihood of both the survival and recovery of grizzly bears."[114]

FWS noted: "Although grizzly bear/livestock conflicts will likely continue and individual grizzly bears may be adversely impacted as a result of the proposed action, the overall core population of grizzly bears of the Greater Yellowstone Ecosystem is expected to remain relatively unaffected by grazing activities in the project area."

FWS determined that while there may be adverse impacts to individual bears, "we do not expect the level of adverse effects to appreciably diminish the numbers, distribution, or reproduction of grizzly bears."

FWS issued an incidental take statement for continued grazing by the Sheep Station, anticipating the loss of no more than three grizzlies in the area within a ten-year period, which would cause "a relatively minor impact on the overall population of this species." FWS concluded that continued sheep grazing would not affect "the survival of grizzly bears nor will it impede recovery."

Casting suspicion on employees of the Sheep Station in the presumed death of the grizzly, anti-grazing groups threatened to sue to shut down livestock grazing if action wasn't taken to protect grizzlies in the area.

Sheep grazing at the Sheep Station continued, with the agency practicing proper food storage and using a fulltime herder and guardian dogs to minimize conflicts with large carnivores, but in late August 2013, a sheepherder shot and killed a male grizzly that was killing sheep near his camp.[115] According to investigative records from FWS law enforcement, the herder's livestock guardian dogs were successful at driving a grizzly bear away from the flock it had attempted to enter during the night. The next morning, three dead and partially-consumed sheep were found, and the herder moved his camp and the flock one mile to the east of that location. Around 2 a.m. the next morning, the grizzly approached the herder's camp, and the guardian dogs once again set upon the bear. When the grizzly bear continued to engage the dogs and became increasingly aggressive, the herder shot the grizzly just fifty yards from his tent. The bear fled into the night, with the dogs following. Sure that the bear had been hit, the herder continued after the wounded bear, killing it 150 yards east of his camp.

The herder reported to his employer that he had killed the bear, and investigators arrived on scene later the same day. A necropsy revealed the bear's stomach was full of sheep meat and wool fibers. When the investigative report was turned over to federal prosecutors for review, it was declined for prosecution by US Attorney's Office, so the case was closed. The grazing activists were outraged.

Anti-grazing group Western Watersheds Project and other groups had a history of litigation over continued operation of the Sheep Station. These groups first filed a lawsuit in 2007, seeking an environmental analysis on effects of livestock grazing, but eventually settling the case when the environmental review went forward. The next lawsuit was in 2013, challenging the 2011 FWS biological opinion that sheep grazing was not likely to jeopardize the grizzly bear population. That case was settled when federal wildlife officials agreed to issue an updated biological opinion by mid-2014 and Sheep Station officials agreed not to graze sheep on three allotments (Summer East, Summer West, and Meyers Creek, including two exclusively on Sheep Station land outside the recovery zone). Then in 2014, the groups once again challenged the Sheep Station's grazing program, and the FWS authorization of one grizzly bear death before the federal agency would need to undergo another review. The case was settled when University of Idaho, citing the ongoing lawsuits, decided not to graze the sheep on Sheep Station-managed lands (Meyers Creek, East, and West) "pending resolution of legal issues and completion of any necessary environmental reviews." Unable to conduct its high elevation grazing research operations, Sheep Station officials agreed not to graze its Summer West range

(also outside the recovery zone) until further environmental review was completed. The anti-grazing groups actions had forced not just the end to sheep grazing within the grizzly bear recovery zone, but to grazing lands outside that zone.

In announcing the most recent agreement not to graze, Bryan Bird of WildEarth Guardians said: "Of course, we're hoping this is more than a temporary closure. The Sheep Station has been problematic for a variety of reasons, from ecological to economic."

By then, many feared the agency had essentially given up, preparing to close the doors on the entire Sheep Station. The station remained open through 2015 only because Congressional action forced it to remain. In a meeting between USDA officials and representatives of the American Sheep Industry Association in early 2014, federal officials complained of the harassing lawsuits against the sheep center, and a month later, ARS proposed to close the facility by the year's end. Domestic sheep industry members across the country rose in opposition to the closure, and Congress directed the station to remain open through the 2015 Fiscal Year. Most believed the closure of the Sheep Station would only be a matter of time—not because of the inability to share the range with grizzly bears, but because grizzly bears were being used as a weapon to destroy the livestock grazing industry. But the Sheep Station plowed forward, soon releasing a revised environmental impact statement proposing that its historic grazing program be allowed to continue. Environmental group challenges are sure to follow.

The federal grizzly bear conservation strategy included habitat standards within the recovery zone, including one calling

Return of the Grizzly

The battle over the future of the Sheep Station continues.

for no net increase in the number of commercial livestock grazing allotments or any increase in permitted sheep numbers within the recovery zone above those in place in 1998. Existing livestock allotments within the zone were to be phased out as the opportunity arose with willing permittees.[116] The Sheep Station's Meyers Creek Allotment was the only active sheep grazing allotment remaining within the grizzly bear recovery zone. The last cattle allotment within Grand Teton National Park was closed in 2011, and by then, the number of active cattle grazing allotments inside the zone had dropped from seventy-two to fifty-four—a permanent closure of nearly 30 percent of the area grazed by cattle within the zone. In 1998, there were also thirteen vacant cattle allotments, and nearly 60 percent of the area encompassed by these allotments was also permanently closed to livestock grazing (sixty square miles).

There were no habitat standards enacted for grizzly bears occurring outside the recovery zone, and although agencies monitor habitat changes, there is no central data collection point to tally the allotments outside the recovery zone that have been closed due to grizzlies. Environmental groups continue to target allotments outside the recovery zone for closure, calling for an ever-increasing region to be off limits to livestock grazing.

CHAPTER 15

DEFINING SUCCESS

A yearling grizzly bear stands up for a better look through the brush.

Wearing a wool sweater and jeans clumsily tucked into the top of his well-worn boots, WG&F bear biologist Zach Turnbull admits he's probably better at reading bears than humans. He speaks with a quiet mannerism, and it's evident that this man is more suited to outdoor life than that of modern society. Raised in Oregon's rural countryside, spending his time hunting, fishing, and trapping, Turnbull eventually came to the Wyoming Game and Fish Department to handle large carnivore conflicts for the agency.

"I never saw a grizzly bear or wolf until I showed up here," he said, although he'd dealt with livestock depredations involving coyotes and mountain lions. "There's no one who ever shows up here who's done this kind of work." At thirty-seven years old, he's handled more than two hundred wild grizzlies, and seems somewhat misplaced from an earlier era. With a .45 caliber revolver strapped to his chest, a can of bear spray on his belt, and a dog in the back of his always-dirty pickup truck, Turnbull spends most days alone in the field, and has probably spent more nights camped in the Upper Green than any modern human on the planet.

"I have literally worn out good knives looking at hundreds of carcasses in Sublette County," he said. "There's not many people in many places who have handled that kind of volume." When large carnivores kill domestic livestock in the Upper Green, or in other areas of Sublette County, Turnbull is often the wildlife specialist who responds to the call, confirming what species was responsible for the killing, and setting traps or snares to catch the offending animal.

"Most of the livestock-killing bears are pretty secret," Turnbull explains. "Ninety-five percent of livestock killing bears, the first time you are going to see them is on a game camera or when they are in a trap."

Once the offending grizzly is trapped, its identifying information is checked for a rap sheet of past offenses, leading agency management decisions whether the bear should be released on site (exclusively for non-target captures), relocated, or euthanized.

"As a wildlife manager I manage species of wildlife, populations of wildlife," Turnbull said. "It is absolutely miserable to start off your day killing a bear. I did not get into wildlife management to kill wildlife in a trap. We look at it as doing what's right for the population, and by getting rid of that really bad individual, you're creating an environment for other bears to succeed."

"When I handle a bear it's never in a good situation," Turnbull said. "Something's gone wrong and it's in a conflict. Sometimes it's bad for people and sometimes it's bad for bears."

Turnbull takes a pragmatic approach to defining success when it comes to relocating grizzly bears. "There are times that I relocate a bear and all I've got to do is just get him out of the situation he's in where I can get something secured or a fence around a beehive. In some situations, all I'm after is buying time." Other times, what he's after is getting the animal away from cattle or sheep.

Defining success is complicated. Turnbull used an example of a grizzly relocated after getting into garbage in a rural subdivision. The bear can go right back to a subdivision and if the garbage has been secured, then the returning bear doesn't get a food reward or have further trouble, and that's a success.

But when a bear that kills livestock in the Upper Green is relocated to a remote location east of Yellowstone park, only to have the bear enter into another area with livestock and once again begin its cattle-killing behavior, then it's not a success and the bear will be permanently removed from the population.

"But there is lots of in between," Turnbull said. For example, if a sow grizzly with cubs gets into trouble and is relocated, and that relocation delays her return to an area until the next year when she is no longer accompanied by her cubs, and then the sow once again gets into trouble and is removed from the population, is that a success or a failure? Since the female is permanently removed from the population, some would consider this a failure, but others would view the fact that she raised her cubs before getting back into trouble a success. Removing one sow is better than having to remove a sow with cubs, in Turnbull's accounting.

"When I set a trap to catch a grizzly bear, I absolutely want to catch that bear if I've made the decision to catch him," Turnbull said. "I'd rather not have that situation have gone wrong—not have that dead calf, or not have that garbage can turned over,

A minority of grizzlies are responsible for a majority of livestock depredations in Wyoming.

whatever. Something's gone wrong at the point I'm involved."

Turnbull's work has changed as the grizzly population has grown. In the past, it appeared that a majority of livestock depredations were the responsibility of a minority of bears, but "today, I think that minority has grown a bit." A few chronic cattle killers were responsible for most damages, but that has changed, as has his approach.

Historically he'd set a trap for up to three nights to get an offending bear, but now he only traps for one night because of the density of grizzlies in the Upper Green. If he can't catch the offending bear the first night, he's not going to be successful, and that's because the program is focused on "targeted removal," meaning that it's aimed at not catching any bear that comes to the

trap set, but instead at catching the offending individual.

Although there appears to be more grizzlies than prey on cattle, there are still a good number of bears that don't deprecate cattle. In Turnbull's opinion, a sow grizzly who kills a calf every few years isn't much of a problem. "We're after the bear that's killing cattle night after night," he explained. "We never quite get all the depredators out by the end of the year."

Those who handle grizzlies follow protocols to reduce the risk of personal injury, and indeed there have been few injuries or deaths to biologists, but when you are in the mountains alone, dealing with a grizzly bear in a snare, personal safety is never guaranteed. Most of the men who undertake jobs such as this one are not willing to go on record about their close calls, but

Return of the Grizzly

as Turnbull says, "We've all had our close calls."

"We do everything that we tell people not to, every single day of the summer and fall season," Turnbull explains, including going alone into the willows where a bear is suspected to be present, setting traps at daylight and dusk, near a carcass that the bear is using as a food source.

"We are professionals. We know what we're doing and we've been doing it a long time so we have a pretty good sense of what's going to work and what's not, what's going to put me in danger and what's not, and the rest of the guys that are managing bears across the ecosystem are the same," he explains. "We give educational talks, and we do all this stuff that you're not supposed to do, and none of us have ever been injured by a bear."

Just about everyone who works in the agency's large carnivore section has been involved in car accidents, plane wrecks, or other accidents, but no one has been injured by a grizzly.

"That says something to our credit, but it also says something to the bear's credit too," Turnbull said, pointing out that there is an incredible amount of interaction that goes on, even though in many cases, people are unaware that a grizzly bear is present.

"I think day-in, day-out, they have more tolerance for people than folks give them credit for," he said. "They are incredibly durable, both as a species and as individuals," adding that grizzlies have been found to live in the badlands in parts of Wyoming inhabited by little else but "cactus and rattlesnakes."

"If your heart doesn't skip a beat when you show up and a bear's in a trap or snare, something's wrong with you," Turnbull said. "But if I never handled another bear for the rest of my life, I'd die happy. There are lots of things I do for fun, and bears aren't one of them."

Grizzlies have more tolerance for people than most people would expect.

Defining Success

CHAPTER 16

CHANGING LANDSCAPE

As the grizzly bear population expanded across the landscape, it brought conflicts between bears and humans in areas that grizzlies hadn't inhabited for decades.

One fall afternoon after most of the cattle had already left their summer grazing pastures in the Upper Green, Albert Sommers and a few other ranchers rode horseback along the Green River, making sure that all the cattle had already moved down the trail. One of the riders found two dead calves down in the willows along an oxbow of the river. Since one of the calves was obviously a grizzly kill, Sommers radioed WG&F to send someone to confirm the kill. The riders went on about their work, but Sommers and Big Piney rancher Eddie Wardell trailered their horses back to the oxbow to meet up with WG&F's Ken Mills. Carrying a shotgun, Mills was on foot, a can of pepper spray strapped to his hip. As the two men on horseback were showing

Mills the two carcasses, they noticed some ravens on another oxbow just to the south.

Thinking there may be another grizzly-killed calf, they decided to go toward the ravens. Sommers described what happened next: "So we started scouting around among these willows, and I pushed into a real thicket, on horseback—one of those thickets that you've got to make your horse get into." His roan mare, Betsey, pushed forward, but Sommers could tell from the way the horses were behaving that they could smell a bear.

"When I got in there, there was a grizzly about fifteen yards—no more than that—out in front of me, on all fours," Sommers said. "When I yelled, 'Bear!' (because Ken Mills was behind me, afoot) . . . that bear just turned and charged. I mean front-legs-coming-over-the-top-of-the-shoulders charge."

"Eddie said I yelled again, and I don't remember that yell—and then me and the horse, we came back out," he said. "The horse didn't like it, I didn't like it, we came back out."

Wardell and Mills were in an opening along the edge of willow patch at the river's shoreline.

"When I came back by, I went right by Eddie Wardell, and when I went by Eddie, Eddie yelled, and I turned my horse around," Sommers said. "Eddie said that bear was about fifteen feet behind me when I came out of that willow patch. When Eddie yelled, I saw the bear stop at the edge of the willows, right in front of Eddie. Ken Mills had dropped his shotgun and was going for his pepper spray. The bear turned at that point when he saw more people, and he lit out back through the willows."

Sommers is thankful that the encounter ended there, with no man or animal injured or killed. Mills had done the right thing by pulling out his bear spray but not deploying it. In that close of conflict, the men and horses would have been sprayed as well as the bear, Sommers said, "and you'd probably had a huge wreck."

Later that fall when Albert and Betsey flushed a moose out of the willows at the ranch, "she about jumped out of her skin.

Riders push cattle up the Green River Drift cattle driveway for summer and fall grazing in the Upper Green.

Changing Landscape

She'd never been like that around a moose before but it was a dark object coming out of the willows." Both man and beast remembered their shared experience.

The cattleman has become accustomed to encounters with grizzlies in the Upper Green, but most of those encounters were while he was on horseback. "I've hit lots of grizzlies with horses, bounced them, and they always run or move away," he said. "I've never had one do that. You could say it was a bluff charge, but it didn't feel like he was bluffing much."

The next day Sommers learned that a group of local ladies had a grizzly bear charge past them the day prior on the other side of the river. "I'm sure that was the same bear."

Sommers said that the cattlemen have changed the way they do things in the Upper Green in response to grizzly bear presence. Since their range monitoring sites are located in the willows, monitoring must be done in teams, with at least one member carrying bear spray. Range riders are trained in food storage and keeping clean camps, and are cautioned not to get off their horses at a depredation site without someone else present, and to "be very, very careful."

"It's the real deal," Sommers said. "You have to pay attention. You do not want to put yourself in a position up there where you could get attacked. You do not want to attract a bear to your camp. There's things you just should not do, and it's a lot different than it used to be."

Despite the constant presence of grizzlies, no range rider has yet to kill a bear, or shoot a bear. No one has been hurt by a grizzly, although riders have been charged on several occasions.

"It's changed entirely how we have to manage because we manage, to a large degree, for the bear," Sommers said. "We look for conflicts. We have to work continually putting cattle back in to places where they've been because they blow out from predators. Management has become about the state of the predator in the pasture. If the predators are quiet, the cattle are quiet."

In 2015, the grass was as tall as a cow's back in some places, but riders couldn't keep the cattle in these areas because of predators. "We couldn't keep cattle in what was the best grass that I've ever seen in my lifetime because they couldn't stand the pressure from the predators."

Sommers has seen recreational use of the Upper Green change with the ever-increasing grizzly population as well. "I just don't think people are comfortable camping up there now like they used to be," he said, and with food storage requirements, people don't tend to picnic in the area as they did in years past.

The Continental Divide Trail that traverses the Upper Green is increasingly used by bicyclists who Sommers feels are generally unaware that they are camping in small tents in one of the highest grizzly bear densities in existence.

"I know that hunters have changed, and that some of them don't want to hunt up there now because they don't want to have to deal with bears," he said. "I've had people tell me that this year." Members of the Wyoming Outfitters and Guides Association that provide hunts outside of the Yellowstone ecosystem now advertise that they offer hunts in areas without grizzly bears.

When the Board of Review Report on Lance Crosby's death was released in January 2016, sixty cattlemen had filled a meeting room in Sublette County, gathered to talk about grizzly bear conflicts in the Upper

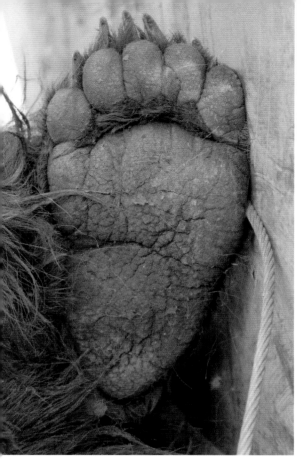

The hind foot of an immobilized adult male grizzly.

Green, brainstorming ways to reduce conflicts between livestock and grizzly bears. This invitation-only workshop was spearheaded by Upper Green River Cattle Association President Albert Sommers, with three environmental organizations providing the logistics for the session, but providing their service silently: this was indeed a cattlemen's meeting. Every cattle producer in the room had scattered hay to their herds that snowy morning before driving to town to attend the session. The situation for cattle in the Upper Green was dire: calf losses from the previous grazing season had reached an all-time high of nearly 14 percent.

Since 1994, WG&F had confirmed a total of more than five hundred cattle depredations on the Upper Green cattle allotments, and had relocated fifty-three grizzly bears, in addition to the twenty-five grizzlies that were permanently removed from the population. In 2015, there were eighty confirmed cattle killed by grizzlies, with nine grizzlies relocated, and seven removed from the population.

"It's really become untenable, in my opinion," Sommers said. "I'm the one who has to deal with it but I may have a different perspective than other ranchers in the association. I'm the one who deals with the riders, and listens to the stories, I'm the one who does the monitoring. I'm the one who has to deal with all that stuff."

"It's too much," he said. "You cannot have predation like we had last year and continue to graze. It's just too much on a bunch of cattle.

"We do not raise cattle to feed bears," Sommers said. "And I really do appreciate the Wyoming Game and Fish Department, and I really appreciate the compensation program, because without that, we would not be in business up there. We could not be in business up there."

Critics say the cattle association needs more range riders and those riders should do things differently somehow. But most depredations occur at night, and the association is not going to send range riders out in the night with flashlights and noise-makers to get themselves hurt.

Agency removals due to grizzly bear conflicts with livestock accounted for nearly 15 percent of known grizzly bear mortalities in the Yellowstone region in the last decade, and 33 percent of management removals (with only one of the forty-five mortalities occurring inside the recovery zone). Federal officials noted that agency management removals are "a necessary component of grizzly bear conservation. Nuisance bears can become a threat to human safety and erode public support if they are not addressed. Without the support of the people that live, work, and recreate in grizzly bear country, conservation will not be successful."[117]

Sommers is working on possible ways to reduce depredations on cattle in the Upper Green, but the road ahead is difficult. "What we need to do is break the cycle of habituation of the bears to cattle killing, because you're not going to retrain a bear that has killed cattle," Sommers said. "It's not going to happen."

After the 2015 grazing season, Sommers said: "We're short 290 calves and there are eighty confirmed kills that are calves and yearlings. If you looked at our dead list and figured out how many pounds that is, it's an enormous buffet."

This level of livestock loss is not sustainable for local ranches, even with compensation from WG&F. Despite the problems, Sommers views the Upper Green as a success story for grizzly bears, since the grizzly bear population had been able to expand its range all the way down both the Wind River and Wyoming mountain ranges in Wyoming—areas not envisioned to become home to grizzlies when recovery efforts first began.

WG&F's Dan Thompson jokingly calls the early days of bear recovery program "the no bear left behind" program, since every effort was made to keep individual bears alive at that time when the population was on the brink. But tireless work by dedicated people to resolve conflicts built the program of recovery that has now shifted to conservation and management. It's Thompson's view that the Upper Green

A grizzly bear approaches a parked vehicle along a state highway in western Wyoming.

Return of the Grizzly

should have both continued livestock grazing and grizzly bears.

"As far as the State of Wyoming is concerned, and as far as I'm concerned, the people of the state have given all they can as far as grizzly bears go. We really don't need to keep going down that road," Thompson said, adding that "the cooperation and sacrifices of the public and producers have got us to the point where we are at now which should be acknowledged and celebrated."

While conflicts between cattle and grizzlies continued, the Upper Green was viewed as a grizzly bear recovery success.

CHAPTER 17

DELISTING DO-OVER

The removal of federal protections for the Yellowstone region's grizzly bear population continues to generate much controversy.

On March 4, 2016, FWS announced it would issue rules removing grizzly bears in the Yellowstone ecosystem from the list of protected species. In a press release announcing the proposal, FWS noted: "The restoration of the grizzly bear in Montana, Wyoming and Idaho during the last three decades stands as one of America's great conservation successes—a testament to the value of the Endangered Species Act and the strong partnerships it drives. The Yellowstone grizzly bear population has rebounded from as few as 136 bears in 1975 to an estimated seven hundred or more today."

In conjunction with releasing the proposal for public review, FWS once again posted a slew of documents, including a new draft conservation strategy, and a new supplement to the recovery plan. At the same time, WG&F released its new proposed grizzly bear management plan for public review. The public was once again inundated with nearly seven hundred pages of new delisting details to review, while environmental groups flooded media with press releases opposed to delisting.

The Sierra Club declared it was "deeply opposed" to the delisting proposal because it "not only fails to preserve the progress made toward bear recovery, it will reverse it. It falls short of maintaining a healthy bear population and leaves bears straying outside Yellowstone and Grand Teton National Parks at the mercy of hostile state management policies."[118] The Humane Society of the United States immediately announced it would fight FWS to keep grizzlies from being managed by the states.[119] The Center for Biological Diversity claimed delisting was a reckless act in which "Feds walk away from Yellowstone's Grizzlies," and warning in a fundraising letter: "If grizzlies lose their legal protection, the minute they step outside of Yellowstone, they could be gunned down."[120]

The Natural Resources Defense Council stated, "Certainly we can all agree that the recovery of grizzly bears in the Yellowstone region has been a tremendous success and has prevented this population from going extinct," but then expressed its opposition to delisting: "Given all of the uncertainty facing this population, we do not think it is time to declare victory for these bears just yet."[121]

Wyoming Wildlife Advocates, a group led by two Jackson Hole wildlife photographers, came out against delisting, claiming that grizzlies were roaming farther to search for replacements for lost pine nuts and trout. "We see little evidence that the states intend to make conflict prevention a priority. After delisting, Montana, Wyoming, and Idaho have pledged to allow the bears to be hunted for sport. This will only add to the annual number of deaths.

"In fact, one of the greatest threats grizzlies face comes from state game and fish agencies which have an inherent conflict of interest between managing game species and sustaining a recovered species that preys on valued game species. The two missions are in direct opposition to each other. . . . We see little evidence that any of the three states will exercise restraint when they initiate grizzly hunts. We are concerned that, without robust oversight from the federal government, the states will once again place the bears in jeopardy."[122]

But the IGBC had long suggested regulated hunting as a method to manage grizzly bear distribution and density once the population had reached recovery levels, pointing to the fact that species recovery is often funded by sportsmen's dollars generated from license sales for hunted species.[123]

Some of the opposition to delisting arose just a few months before the proposal was announced when the Associated Press revealed that the three states of the Yellowstone region had drafted a memorandum regarding the management of "discretionary mortality" of grizzlies in the region. This was defined as the amount of human-caused mortality over which agencies have discretionary authority, "such as management removals and regulated harvest." Critics immediately raised cries of alarm at the possibility that grizzly bears could be hunted upon delisting, but regulated hunting of grizzlies was an action that had was anticipated and planned for decades. Still, Wayne Pacelle of The Humane Society of the United States wrote that this was a "dangerous delegation of power to states" that were "displaying an irrational and frightening exuberance for authorizing trophy-hunting programs for this threatened species."[124]

Most of controversy over delisting grizzlies centered on the possibility that a limited number of grizzlies could be hunted in areas outside the national parks.

Included in the delisting proposal were strict mortality quotas and prohibitions on the killing of females with young, as well as provisions to manage for sustaining a population of 674 grizzlies in the region—174 bears more than the minimum called for in the recovery plan. The agreement specified that if the population dropped below six hundred grizzlies, discretionary mortality would not be allowed—except for cases involving human safety.

The 674-bear number marked the average population from 2002 to 2014, when bear officials believe the population stabilized. FWS noted once again that the Yellowstone region's grizzly bear population had reached its long-term carrying capacity, but bear advocates defiantly disputed the claim.

The new conservation strategy maintained the overall goals presented in the original strategy proposed back in 2007:

- The Primary Conservation Area (PCA) would serve as a secure area for grizzly bears, with population and habitat conditions maintained to ensure a recovered population is maintained for the foreseeable future and to allow bears to continue to expand outside the PCA.

- Outside of the PCA, grizzly bears would be allowed to expand into biologically suitable and socially acceptable areas.

- Outside of the PCA, the objective would be to maintain existing resource management and recreational uses

Return of the Grizzly

and to allow agencies to respond to demonstrated problems with appropriate management actions.

- Outside of the PCA, the key to successful management of grizzly bears lies in bears utilizing lands that are not managed solely for bears but in which their needs are considered along with other uses.

The strategy called for a minimum population of five hundred grizzlies, at least forty-eight females with cubs, and occupation of sixteen of the nineteen bear management units, as well as mortality limits on independent females, independent males, and dependent young. According to the strategy, "These adjustable mortality rates were calculated as those necessary to manage the population to the model average of 674 bears which occurred during the time period that this population's growth stabilized."

Two of the most vocal critics of the delisting scheme are the husband-wife team of David Mattson and Louisa Willcox of Montana. Willcox has been a grizzly bear activist for more than thirty years, holding positions with the Sierra Club, Greater Yellowstone Coalition, Natural Resources Defense Council, and finally, with husband Mattson, as founder of the Grizzly Times website (www.grizzlytimes.org/). Mattson, previously a member of the Interagency Grizzly Bear Study Team (until he publicly challenged the science driving delisting) maintains that the catastrophic loss of whitebark pine seeds and cutthroat trout had resulted to grizzlies turning to more meat consumption, resulting in increases in bear deaths as they conflict with livestock and hunters. Mattson alleged that the grizzly bear population "has not grown since the early 2000s and may have even declined

since 2007," an allegation refuted by the IGBST.[125]

For a sample of the views expressed on Grizzly Times, the pair posted a "Debunking Delisting" piece that states, "Governors and appointed state wildlife commissioners have drawn the covered wagons of control in a circle and are shooting outward at anyone non-white, non-fundamentalist Christian, non-hunter, and yes, even non-male—anyone who questions their values of domination."[126]

In a posting on Counterpunch.org shortly after the delisting proposal was announced, Willcox predicted that without federal protections, Yellowstone's grizzlies would likely be pushed back to the brink of extinction because grizzlies would be managed by "anti-carnivore states."[127]

Mattson went even further, writing on Counterpunch that "wildlife management by the states of Wyoming, Idaho and Montana is a corrupt and despotic system enslaved through culture and financial dependencies to serving the interests of those who have a worldview that features violence, iconizes weapons, makes fetishes of sexual organs, and instrumentalizes animals. Moreover, state wildlife managers have a history of demonizing carnivores in defiance of the best available science . . ."[128]

Once a grizzly bear advocate who focused on science, Willcox called Wyoming's bear managers "Wyoming's thugs," and claimed that "cattlemen are complaining ever more loudly about grizzly depredations on typically ill-managed livestock" in the Upper Green River region. Willcox's view ignores the fact that the reason why the Upper Green has one of the highest grizzly bear densities in the lower forty-eight is because of the good work of bear managers and cattle producers, dealing with very difficult and dangerous situations.

Willcox continued to take shots at the Upper Green cattlemen, calling the Upper Green a "black hole" for grizzlies. In addition to outright name-calling, Willcox put forth vile claims in her opinion pieces, such as: "Livestock husbandry in the Upper Green tends to be slovenly, even cynical, with sick calves left un-doctored so that when a bear kills them, the state of Wyoming pays them more than fair market value—a practice that some call 'baiting.'" Rather than limiting argument to the merits of delisting, bear advocacy had degenerated to demonizing those with different views, and perpetuating falsehoods.

When Bridger-Teton National Forest officials issued environmental documents proposing to reauthorize livestock grazing in the Upper Green, bear advocates were outraged that forest officials rejected their "bear-friendly" grazing plan due to the fact that the effectiveness of the proposal was questionable.

Other bear advocates, including the Humane Society of the United States, attempted to equate delisting with immediate trophy hunting of grizzlies. This national organization commissioned a public opinion poll with questions such as:

Should Yellowstone's grizzly bears lose their Endangered Species Act protections, management of these animals revert to Idaho, Montana and Wyoming who have stated they will open up a trophy hunting season. Do you agree or disagree that there should be at least a five-year moratorium on trophy hunting to ensure that the population is fully recovered?

Once delisted, it is possible that state managers could allow Yellowstone area grizzly bears to be hunted by the following methods—hounding—where participants release packs of radio-collared dogs to chase bears into trees—and baiting, where piles of rotten and junk foods are placed in a certain location to lure bears for an easy kill at point blank range. Do you support or oppose allowing trophy hunters to use these methods to kill Yellowstone area grizzly bears?[129]

Bear managers regarded hunting as a method to discourage grizzly bear presence near residences and human developments, and to reduce grizzly densities in localized areas. But hunting bears with hounds in Wyoming is not legal under state statute, and where bear baiting is allowed, the baits must be in sealed containers—not "piles of rotten and junk foods" as suggested by the Humane Society poll. Wyoming law does not allow hunters to use bait for black bear hunting in many areas due to grizzly bears, and if a grizzly bear shows up at a black bear bait, that bait site it must be closed to hunting for the remainder of the season.

As bear researcher Stephen Herrero wrote: "Hunting most species results in animals that avoid people, at least during the hunting season. Unhunted populations usually accept people at closer distances before fleeing. Hunting is one potential means of changing grizzly bear behavior so that surviving bears avoid people."[130] But the scientific reasons behind the potential for hunting never made it into public discussion.

In fact, the greatest source of grizzly bear mortality in the Yellowstone ecosystem during the previous decade had been from interactions with hunters, mostly in surprise encounters, at big game carcasses or hunter camps.[131] Yet during that same

Return of the Grizzly

time, the number of ungulate hunters in grizzly bear habitat decreased, as sportsmen decided to take their hunting pursuits outside of grizzly bear range.

A 2015 investigation by *Jackson Hole News and Guide* reporter Mike Koshmrl found that about 60 percent of the hunter-caused grizzly deaths in the previous decade involved scenarios "in which hunters had only moments to respond, and fired their weapons at charging or menacingly close grizzlies within seconds of seeing them." The other 40 percent of the time "hunters weren't surprised by the grizzlies they shot, but, rather, saw them from a ways off, had reason to be on guard or were trying to deal with problem-causing bears."[132]

FWS received more than sixty-three thousand comments on the delisting proposal documents, but the debate had become an emotion-filled spectacle, full of drama but nearly devoid of real substance. It would take the federal agency months to dig through all the comments.

The Yellowstone Ecosystem Subcommittee (YES) established a steering committee to work through revision of the conservation strategy, and that group met at least once a month through 2016 in attempt to comply with the FWS's desire to publish a final rule on delisting grizzlies in the Yellowstone region by the end of the year. Yellowstone National Park Superintendent Dan Wenk pointed out at the April session that the timeline was clearly ambitious, and added that the National Park Service had concerns with major components of the strategy. But FWS wanted the group to restrict its edits only to the extent necessary to address changes in the recovery criteria and new science.

Those who opposed delisting claimed that the grizzly population would suffer under state management – a notion contested by state wildlife officials.

Delisting Do-Over

It became apparent that Wenk's concerns focused on the potential harvest of grizzlies (discretionary mortality). Wenk didn't want bears harvested in close proximity to the park, and advocated a prohibition on hunting bears within the John D. Rockefeller Jr. Memorial Parkway connecting Grand Teton and Yellowstone. The parkway is managed as a National Park Service unit, but the enabling legislation for the parkway allows hunting at the discretion of the Wyoming Game and Fish Commission. The National Park Service also wanted the level of discretionary mortality to be based on the number of grizzly bears located outside the national parks rather the entire population, and wanted to have a decision-making seat at the interagency table with state wildlife managers as they discuss discretionary mortalities even after delisting occurred. Wenk also pointed out that the population estimator used by bear managers was conservative (indicating there may be about seven hundred bears when in reality there was probably more than one thousand bears in the population), so if another population size estimator was adopted in the future, mortality limits should be adjusted as well. For example, if a new estimator determined that there were one thousand bears in the population, Wenk didn't want the states to authorize the harvest of two hundred to three hundred bears.

During the group's July conference call, Wenk emphasized the view that Yellowstone should not be a source population to provide bears for the states to hunt. WG&F representative Brian Nesvik pointed out that the grizzly bear population is managed at the ecosystem level and that while bears would routinely move throughout the ecosystem, none of the discretionary mortalities would occur within the national parks.

Nesvik urged the committee to continue its discussion of biological issues, but Wenk continued to balk, noting that harvest of bears was a difficult issue for the national parks and state officials to come to terms on, and the park service wanted park visitors to continue to view grizzlies within the parks. When a committee member questioned whether the conservation strategy (a science-based document) was the appropriate venue for the NPS concerns—which were related to "optics," Wenk responded that if it were up to him, it would be in the rules.

Nesvik pointed out that the states have a conservation-based mission, but the NPS has a preservation-based mission, and that both could achieve their missions under the conservation strategy. Wenk acknowledged that this wasn't a scientific issue, but remained a major concern for his agency and its constituents.

Both Forest Service and county commission representatives pointed out that some of the commitment suggestions brought forth seemed to be based on continuing management of a listed species, rather than post-delisting management of a recovered species.

Although the group continued to meet and discuss these issues in the following months, Wenk ended up casting the lone vote in opposition to moving forward with the conservation strategy at a November 2016 meeting. All the other committee members—from county commissioners and state officials, national forest representatives, to other federal agencies, including Wenk's Grand Teton National Park counterpart—voted to support the strategy. Delisting was poised to move forward.

CHAPTER 18

AN UNEASY CO-EXISTENCE

Visitors traveling to national parks in western Wyoming expect to see grizzly bears, and most succeed in doing so—even though the grizzly bear was still listed as a threatened species.

When the major tourism season began in May 2016, it quickly became clear that the masses flocking to the Yellowstone region were clueless as to how to behave in the great outdoors. The problems started with a woman being filmed as she petted the head of a resting adult bison in Yellowstone National Park, and another visitor was fined and placed on probation for placing a newborn bison calf in his vehicle because he feared for its welfare. Although park officials attempted to place the bison calf back with its herd, the animal was rejected and later euthanized. The woman who petted the bison had escaped injury, but she was lucky since bison injure more park visitors than any other wild animal—including five visitors the previous year.

Next, four Canadian men traveling across America filming videos of their adventures—including one in which they ventured off the boardwalks at Grand Prismatic Spring in Yellowstone—illegally trampled in the hot springs area. By the time the US Attorney's Office filed misdemeanor charges against the men, they were safely back in Canada.

Some visitors ignore the posted multi-lingual warning signs about the dangers of the hydrothermal features that can be viewed from the surface ("Leaving the boardwalk . . . is unlawful and potentially fatal"), and thus several people were scalded just a month into the summer season, including one man who lost his life when he ventured several hundred yards off the boardwalk and fell into the boiling hot springs at Norris Geyser Basin. There was nothing left of his body to recover.

Many visitors are drawn to Yellowstone for its amazing views of hot springs, scalding mudpots, and geysers—features of one of the world's largest active volcanoes that is hidden below. Throughout the season, visitors continued to ignore cautions about approaching wildlife closely, and early in the season, a cow elk knocked a woman down after approaching closely for a photograph. A woman photographing birds at a roadside nest stepped backwards into the lane of traffic and was killed. Park visitation continued to rise, as the National Park Service celebrated its centennial, and *National Geographic* issued its May 2016 edition devoted exclusively to Yellowstone. That month nearly 445,000 people visited Yellowstone National Park, including almost six hundred busloads of tourists. Grand Teton National Park was experiencing record numbers of visitors as well, with nearly 300,000 visitors in the month of May as roadside grizzly bears became a daily draw with hundreds of people parked on the roadsides for viewing.

With low gas prices during the major summer travel season, the pressure didn't

Travelers stop to watch a roadside bear in Wyoming.

Return of the Grizzly

let up. On the same day in June 2016, two bears were killed in hit-and-run accidents in Grand Teton, including one adult black bear and one grizzly bear cub. The cub was the only cub of Bear 399, the twenty-year-old roadside matriarch. Bear advocates were devastated, holding a prayer vigil and roadside memorial for the cub.

At the same time people were rushing to Grand Teton and Yellowstone to see their famous bears, some of the visitors drove right by others. The US Forest Service installed an electric sign along a stretch of US Highway 26/287 between Grand Teton and Dubois, Wyoming, warning motorists of "Bears on Road" as at least one grizzly had become a roadside bear, far outside the safety of a national park.

But habituated grizzlies were becoming a problem on a much larger scale. A grizzly repeatedly approached and charged hikers in Alaska's Denali National Park over a period of weeks in June before finally biting a woman. In Montana, a thirty-eight-year-old mountain biker was killed after colliding with a grizzly that then attacked and killed him in the Flathead National Forest, just outside Glacier National Park. At the time, Canada's Banff National Park was suffering from the same bear jams and problems as Yellowstone, Grand Teton, and Glacier National Parks. In early July, Banff officials warned visitors to use added caution on the Bourgeau Lake Trail after a large grizzly followed two hikers down the trail, even as the group encountered other hikers and added to their group's size. The bear continued to follow what eventually became a group of nine people.

Wildfires blazed throughout western Wyoming through the summer and fall in 2016, including multiple fires in both

A portable sign warns drivers of bears on the roadway in Wyoming.

An Uneasy Co-Existence

Grand Teton and Yellowstone, resulting in road closures and travel restrictions. Even so, park visitation numbers rose above the record levels of the prior year.

In the summer of 2016, the food storage order for the Shoshone and Bridger-Teton National Forests was expanded once again, to include all of national forest lands in western Wyoming with the exception of the Wyoming and Salt River mountain ranges south of The Rim.

In mid-July, Wyoming Game and Fish Department officials trapped and euthanized two male grizzlies that raided garbage cans, prowled through yards, and sorted through the contents of the backs of pickup trucks in an area east of Dubois. The bears were brothers, and ended up raiding about a dozen garbage cans a night, despite state efforts to get garbage and other attractants secured. Their mother had been euthanized the year prior for the same behavior. Research has indicated that development of conflict behaviors may be the result of social learning between mothers and their cubs. Canadian researchers found, "Offspring of problem mothers are more likely to be involved in incidents or human-bear conflicts themselves." The researchers emphasized that preventing sow bears from becoming problem bears would help prevent the perpetuation of conflicts through social learning.[133] They noted: "Social learning has the potential to perpetuate grizzly bear conflicts—highlighting the importance of preventing initial conflicts, but also removing problem individuals once conflicts start. Prompt removal (i.e., culling) of grizzly bears engaged in conflict behavior might be an effective solution for reducing conflicts. . . ."[134]

In response to continued cattle depredations, wildlife managers killed three adult grizzlies (one male and two females) throughout the summer of 2016 in the Upper Green.

In mid-September, an elk hunter was mauled by a grizzly bear twenty-five miles northeast of Jackson. Two weeks later, another hunter survived a grizzly bear attack in southwestern Montana, and a day later, another hunter was attacked while attempting to recover an elk carcass northwest of Dubois, Wyoming.

By the time grizzly bears entered their winter dens in late 2016, there had been fifty-eight grizzly bear deaths in the Yellowstone ecosystem, including natural mortality, human-caused deaths, and probable mortalities. More than a third of the mortalities occurred outside the official demographic monitoring area where bear managers maintain grizzlies are more prone to conflict situations in a human-dominated landscape, and most of these bears were adult males. Eight of the deaths were bears that were killed on highways. Three adult male grizzlies died in separate incidents by drowning in a concrete irrigation canal on private property in Park County, Wyoming. It was a record year for grizzly bear deaths, but with grizzlies very visible throughout the ecosystem, it appeared the bear population was bursting at its seams.

Domestic sheep flocks grazed western Wyoming's Bridger-Teton National Forest for more than a hundred years, but when flocks belonging to the Thoman family ranch came out of the mountains at the end of September 2016, the book closed for domestic sheep in the northern portion of the Bridger-Teton.

Long pressured by environmental groups and federal officials, the Thomans at last conceded, waiving their Elk Ridge Allotment Complex grazing permit back to the

The Thoman family's fine-wooled Rambouillet ewes and lambs stand in pens, leaving the Upper Green for the last time.

Bridger-Teton National Forest without preference to another livestock producer. The deal involved a buyout (of an undisclosed sum) of the allotments. The Thoman's fine-wooled Rambouillets had grazed this range for forty years.

Citing the potential threat of interactions between domestic sheep and wild sheep, and the history of wolf and grizzly bear depredations, Bridger-Teton National Forest officials committed to prohibiting domestic sheep on the allotments. The agency indicated it may consider allowing the currently permitted cattle grazing in the Upper Green to spread into a portion of the Thoman allotments "in order to better address ongoing predation issues," but not until further environmental review is conducted some years in the future.

The loss of the Thoman allotments—four allotments that grazed up to a total of 3,900 sheep from July through September—was the latest in a series of domestic sheep allotment closures by federal forest officials throughout the West. The decision to give up the allotments was a difficult one, and members of the Thoman family voiced displeasure. Family matriarch Mickey Thoman and daughter Mary said they believe that the situation had become such that it was best to accept the buyout offer and put their days in the Upper Green behind them.

"I feel in my heart the timing is now or never," Mary said. "They are running us in the ground."

The Thomans had spent decades trying to comply with ever-increasing burdensome federal regulations and operating instruc-

An Uneasy Co-Existence   – 157 –

tions, while adjusting their operations in an attempt to minimize conflicts with recovering grizzly bear and gray wolf populations. For instance, when grizzly depredations continued to rise despite the presence of herders and guardian dogs, Mary took the initiative to begin the use of portable electric pens for the sheep at night. That voluntary action evolved into a mandatory program in which the pens were required every night, and every detail of their use—from how many panels to voltage, from location restrictions to pen movement every night—was determined by the federal agency.

"We're going to go bankrupt, how much more trying can we do?" Mary asked, noting that federal officials could claim that the Thomans weren't forced off their allotments, but cooperative efforts from agency officials over the years could be classified as half-hearted at best, and hostile at worst.

"We've learned how to deal with bears and wolves, but the bureaucrats I haven't figured out," Mary said.

In the summer of 2017, after more than forty years of federal protection, the Yellowstone region's grizzly bear population was removed from the US list of threatened and endangered species. The Interagency Grizzly Bear Study Team would continue to monitor the population for the next five years, but state wildlife agencies were finally in charge of management, at least until the half-dozen lawsuits challenging the decision were decided by a federal court.

Wyoming Game and Fish Department Large Carnivore Section Supervisor Dan Thompson provided an update on grizzly bear conflicts in early 2017, noting that the increasing grizzly bear distribution throughout the ecosystem had resulted

A sow grizzly with yearling cubs moves across the landscape.

Return of the Grizzly

in greater bear distribution than suitable habitat within the demographic monitoring area (DMA). There has also been a shift in conflicts, with many more livestock attacks than in the past, as well as an increasing number of human injuries and deaths.[135]

Conflict Type	2004-2009	2010-2015
Property Damage	163	83
Livestock Conflict	95	271
Garbage	51	95
Grizzly Bear Deaths	26	16
Human Injury/Death	8	14

State wildlife agencies had a busy summer and fall in 2017, with a total of fifty-six dead bears by year's end.[136] Eleven grizzlies were killed in self-defense situations, including one shot by an off-duty game warden, and three cases involving sows with three young cubs at their sides. There were four cases of grizzly bear-inflicted human injury. Three grizzly deaths were road kills, and two were cases of mistaken identity by black bear hunters. Eight grizzlies were killed because of repeated livestock depredations (including four in the Upper Green) and bear managers removed eight bears after their involvement in conflicts such as approaching developed areas, and exhibiting human habituation. Two other grizzly bear deaths were recorded after they were killed and eaten by other bears, including a cub and an adult female.

Bear managers in the tri-state area began the process of considering whether to hold grizzly bear hunts in 2018. With agreed-to guidelines, Montana would be able to harvest one grizzly, but in the end, declined to hold a hunting season. Idaho decided to move ahead with a season for the harvest of one male bear. Wyoming's proposal caused

outrage because it would allow nearly two-dozen grizzlies to be harvested by hunters. But the state had carefully structured the hunt proposal so that up to one female bear and ten male bears could be taken in a region outside the national parks, but within the DMA. The hunting season would open September 15, and would close immediately if a female grizzly was killed, or if ten male grizzlies were killed, or November 15, whichever came first. All hunters would have mandatory hunter safety and grizzly bear ecology training, and only one hunter would be allowed in the field at a time. In what appears to be a world first, each hunter would be equipped with an electronic tracking device to notify wildlife officials if a grizzly bear was killed.

In order to satisfy those who feared their favorite roadside bears might be killed, Wyoming included a buffer zone east of Grand Teton National Park and the John D. Rockefeller Memorial Parkway to protect these famous bears, and banned hunting within a quarter mile of any state or federal highway. Hunters would not be able to use baits, dogs, traps, radio-telemetry, or snares.

Wyoming's hunting regulations also addressed the area outside the DMA where many grizzly-human conflicts occur, called Hunt Area 7. A total of twelve grizzlies could be harvested from this huge region, and the use of baits could be approved depending on the circumstance. The idea of killing that many bears drew the ire of environmental groups and bear advocates still calling for federal protection for the region's bear population, and smarting from the federal decision that grizzlies occurring outside the DMA do not count towards recovery goals. Federal plans called for maintaining a minimum population of five hundred grizzlies within the DMA, and the official minimum count was over seven hundred bears—not including those bears that occur outside the DMA.

The final rule removing federal protection for bears addressed this issue: "While it is true that the current distribution of grizzly bears extends outside of the DMA into unsuitable habitat, the records of grizzly bears in these areas are generally due to recorded grizzly bear–human conflicts or to transient animals, not reproductive females with offspring. For instance, between 1985 and 2014, only 2.1 percent of all sightings of unduplicated females with cubs-of-the-year were outside of the DMA. These areas are defined as unsuitable due to the high risk of mortality resulting from these grizzly bear–human conflicts. These unsuitable habitat areas do not permit grizzly bear reproduction or survival because bears that repeatedly come into conflict with humans or livestock are usually either relocated or removed from these areas."[137]

While arguments were being made in federal court over the removal of federal protection for grizzlies in the Yellowstone region in the spring of 2018, grizzlies emerged from their winter dens and went about life. Bear-watchers in the Jackson Hole region were elated when the twenty-two-year-old grizzly sow 399 brought her two yearling cubs out for public viewing along the shores of Jackson Lake in Grand Teton National Park in early May.[138]

But the bear news wasn't as positive in other parts of the Northern Rockies. In mid-May, a US Fish and Wildlife Service seasonal field worker for the grizzly bear program was mauled by a bear in Montana's Cabinet Mountains, leaving her with a fractured skull and other injuries. The young woman managed to use her bear spray to stop the attack, then walked several miles to her work vehicle to find help.[139] Before the month ended, Wyoming wildlife officials were investigating the first of the year's self-defense killing of a sow grizzly southwest of Cody. The sow had three cubs at her side when a person had a surprise encounter with the group, but state officials were unable to locate the cubs.[140] State officials killed two other adult male grizzlies after repeated livestock depredations and bold behavior toward humans in locations outside the DMA. It was shaping up to be another year of continued conflict and controversy involving grizzlies, no matter which government agency was charged with managing the species.

WG&F's Zach Turnbull voiced the views of many bear managers in stating that the Endangered Species Act "is certainly a magnificent tool for recovering species, but it's a miserable tool to manage a species that's recovered. That's really what delisting's about—to give bear managers the tools to manage species properly, and as good as they can. It's not about hunting, or about killing every bear that kills a calf. All those other uses of grizzly bears, including photography, will still be there. All those opportunities will still be there."

By the time grizzly bears were removed from the list of federally protected species in 2017, grizzlies occurred across a range of sixteen million acres in the Yellowstone region—an area larger than the state of West Virginia. More than 60 percent of occupied grizzly bear range in the Yellowstone ecosystem occurs outside the original grizzly bear recovery zone. From the early recovery plan's goals of fifteen adult females with young in a minimum population of 158 bears in a 9,200-square-mile recovery zone, there were now at least fifty-eight sows in a population of up to one thousand bears inhabiting more than twenty-five thousand square miles.

And still, some claim that is not enough.

"Ultimately, the future of the grizzly bear will be based on the people who live, work, and recreate in grizzly bear habitat and the willingness and ability of these people to learn to coexist with the grizzly bear and to accept this animal as a cohabitant of the land."

—Federal Register, March 11, 2016. Proposed Rule: Removing the Greater Yellowstone Ecosystem Population of Grizzly Bears from the federal list of Endangered and Threatened Species.

Both humans and animals continue to adjust to the return of the grizzly across vast landscapes in the Greater Yellowstone region.

1

ACKNOWLEDGMENTS

I offer appreciation and gratitude to those contributing to grizzly bear research and management in the Yellowstone ecosystem over the last forty years. From involved citizens and county commissions, to state and federal wildlife managers, your efforts have led to one of our nation's greatest conservation success stories: recovery of the Yellowstone ecosystem's grizzly bear population. That the Yellowstone grizzly bear is one of the most studied mammals on the planet served to my benefit, and I thank the responsible researchers who provided a bounty of information for me to glean from scientific journals. I am especially indebted to numerous Wyoming Game and Fish Department bear managers who tolerated my incessant questions over the decades as I reported for the *Pinedale Roundup* and the *Sublette Examiner*, and for this and other books.

While recovery of a threatened species is a noble endeavor, a cornerstone of grizzly bear management has been the acknowledgement that grizzlies share the ecosystem with human beings. Grizzly bear recovery would not have been achieved without the efforts and tolerance of the human community that shares this wild landscape with a top predator. May we long continue to share the same range.

GREATER YELLOWSTONE GRIZZLIES MEETING THE RECOVERY CRITERIA[141]

Prior to 2013, population parameters such as females with young were only counted for grizzlies that occurred within the official recovery zone/conservation management area—no matter how many grizzlies occurred outside this zone. But bear managers changed the monitoring protocol in 2013 to incorporate grizzlies that occur within the area defined as suitable grizzly habitat, called the Demographic Monitoring Area. Even with the much larger monitoring zone, grizzly sows with cubs outside this zone are not counted toward population monitoring protocols. In 2014, there were three sows with young confirmed outside the DMA.

Recovery Criteria 1: Maintenance of a total population of at least five hundred, with at least forty-eight females with cubs of the year (COY).

Status: 2015 estimated population size: 714. The number of females with COY has not dropped below forty-eight since 2007.

FEMALES W/COY

1973	14 w/26
1983	13 w/22
1993	20 w/41 (including one more than ten miles outside the recovery zone)
2003	38 w/75 (including three more than ten miles outside the recovery zone)
2013	58 w/126

Recovery Criteria 2: Occupancy of sixteen of eighteen Bear Management Units (BMUs) by females with young.

Status: This criterion has been met since 1999.

BMUs Occupied by Females with young

1998	14
2000	17
2005	18
2010	18
2014	18

Recovery Criteria 3: Total mortality limit for independent females may not exceed 9 percent for two consecutive years.

Status: Under threshold.

Recovery Criteria 4: Total mortality limits for independent males may not exceed 15 percent.

Status: Under threshold.

Recovery Criteria 5: The human-caused mortality limit for dependent young may not exceed 9 percent for three consecutive years.

Status: Under threshold.

The bear population's mortality levels remain below federal thresholds.

APPENDIX B:

THE BEAR FACTS: GREATER YELLOWSTONE ECOSYSTEM GRIZZLY DATA

Grizzly Bear Occupancy (square miles)[142]	
1979	6,178
1989	8,880
1999	12,741
2010	19,305
2014	22,394
2016	25,038

Weights:
Average adult male: 413 pounds
Average adult female: 269 pounds
Heaviest male: 715 pounds
Heaviest female: 436 pounds

Area Occupied in GYE:
Twenty-five thousand square miles, an area about the size of the state of West Virginia, with Yellowstone National Park consisting of only about 3,400 square miles of that amount.

Grizzly bears were placed on the federal list of threatened species in 1975. They have not been hunted in the Yellowstone region since 1974, although Wyoming classifies the species as a trophy game animal. The bruins, which weigh from 250 to 600 pounds, live to be thirty to forty years old, although in the Yellowstone region, the oldest bears recorded were from twenty-eight to thirty-one years old. Females usually produce their first litter when they are five years old, and after produce cubs an average of every three years.

Grizzlies are larger than black bears, have long, curved claws, humped shoulders, and a concave face. In coloration, bears range from light brown to nearly black. Grizzlies mate in late May through mid-July, and delayed implantation sets the birth of the one to four cubs near in early February. The bruins hibernate generally from late November through March.

ACRONYMS

ACM   Army cutworm moth
BMA   Bear Management Area
BMU   Bear Management Unit
COY   Cub(s) of the year
DMA   Demographic Monitoring Area
FWS   US Fish and Wildlife Service
GYE   Greater Yellowstone Ecosystem
IGBC   Interagency Grizzly Bear Committee
IGBST   Interagency Grizzly Bear Study Team
PCA   Primary Conservation Area/Recovery Zone
YES   Yellowstone Ecosystem Subcommittee
YNP   Yellowstone National Park
WG&F   Wyoming Game and Fish Department

ENDNOTES

1 Unless otherwise noted, all details of the bear attack on Lance Crosby are found in Board of Review Report—Fatality of Mr. Lance Crosby from a bear attack on Elephant Back Mountain in Yellowstone National Park on August 6, 2015, Chaired by Chris Servheen, US Fish and Wildlife Service Grizzly Bear Recovery Coordinator.

2 Glen F. Cole. "Preservation and Management of Grizzly Bears in Yellowstone National Park." *BioScience*, Vol. 21, No. 16 (Aug. 15, 1971), pp. 858–864.

3 Mary Meagher. "Bears in Transition: 1959-1970s," in *Yellowstone Science* 16(2) (2008): 5–12.

4 John J. Craighead. "Status of the Yellowstone Grizzly Bear Population: Has it recovered, should it be delisted?" *Ursus* 10 (1998): 597–602.

5 50 CFR Part 17 Federal Register, Vol. 40, No. 1, January 2, 1975.

6 Kerry A. Gunther. "Bear Management in Yellowstone National Park," 1960–1993. *Int. Conf. Bear Res. And Management* 9(1) (1994):549–560.

7 Mary Meagher and Jerry R. Phillips. "Restoration of natural populations of grizzly and black bears in Yellowstone National Park." *Bears: Their Biology and Management* (1983): 152–158.

8 John H. Hoak, Tim W. Clark, and John L. Weaver. "Of grizzly bears and commercial outfitters in Bridger-Teton National Forest, Wyoming." *Bears: Their Biology and Management* (1983): 110–117.

9 Gunther, Kerry A., 1994. "Bear Management in Yellowstone National Park, 1960–1993." *Int. Conf. Bear Res. And Management* 9(1):549–560.

10 Colin M. Gillin, F. M. Hammond, and C. M. Peterson. "Aversive Conditioning of Grizzly Bears" in *Yellowstone Science* Vol. 3, Number 1, (1995).

11 Lee H. Whittlesey. *Death in Yellowstone: Accidents and Foolhardiness in the First National Park*. New York: Roberts Rinehart Publishers, 2014.

12 Yellowstone National Park. 1988 Fires. http://home.nps.gov/yell/learn/nature/1988fires.htm, accessed Feb. 23, 2016.

13 Kerry A. Gunther. "Nature Notes: Fire, Smoke and Grizzly Bears." *Yellowstone Science* 17(2) (2009): 45–48.

14 R. R. Knight, and B. M. Blanchard. "Yellowstone Grizzly Bear Investigations: Annual report of the Interagency Grizzly Bear Study Team, 1995." National Biological Service, Bozeman, Montana.

15 M. A. Haroldson, C .C. Schwartz, and K. A. Gunther. "Grizzly Bears in the Greater Yellowstone Ecosystem." *Yellowstone Science* 16(2) (2008): 13–24.

16 C. A. Anders, M. A. Ternent, D. D. Moody. "Grizzly Bear-Cattle Interactions on Two Grazing Allotments in Northwest Wyoming." *Ursus* 13 (2002):247–256.

17 G. M. Holm, F. G. Lindzey, and D. D Moody. "Interactions of sympatric black and grizzly bears in northwest Wyoming." *Ursus* 11 (1999):99–108.

18 National Wildlife Federation press release: "Swapping Conflict for Conservation." Feb. 01, 2004.

19 Interagency Grizzly Bear Guidelines. 1986.

20 L. L. Eberhardt, and R. R. Knight. "How many grizzlies in Yellowstone?" *The Journal of Wildlife Management* (1996): 416–421.

21 Cat Urbigkit. "Grizzly Habitat Needs Next on FWS Agenda." *Pinedale Roundup*, June 12, 1997.

22 Jill Johnson. "Bear Gets Snared." *Pinedale Roundup*. August 7, 1997.

23 Cat Urbigkit. "WG&F Delays Bear Decision." *Pinedale Roundup*. March 5 ,1998.

24 Cat Urbigkit. "Grazing, Grizzlies Conflict." *Pinedale Roundup*. September 25, 1997.

25 Cat Urbigkit. "Grizzlies, Grazing Get Okay." *Pinedale Roundup*. June 24, 1999.

26 Cat Urbigkit. "Stock Killer Destroyed." *Pinedale Roundup*. July 15, 1999.

27 "Grizzly Bear-Human Conflicts, Confrontations, and Management Actions in the Yellowstone Ecosystem." Interagency Grizzly Bear Committee Yellowstone Ecosystem Subcommittee Report. 1999.

28 Cat Urbigkit. "Groups Attack Grizzly Control." *Pinedale Roundup*. Sept. 9, 1999.

29 Cat Urbigkit. "Stock-Killing Bears Released in Sunlight Basin. "*Pinedale Roundup*. Sept. 9, 1999.

30 Cat Urbigkit. "What are we going to do with problem bears?" *Pinedale Roundup*. Sept. 16, 1999.

31 "Grizzly Bear-Human Conflicts, Confrontations, and Management Actions in the Yellowstone Ecosystem." 1999. Interagency Grizzly Bear Committee Yellowstone Ecosystem Subcommittee Report.

32 C. Servheen. "The Grizzly Bear Recovery Program: Current Status and Future Considerations." *Ursus* 10 (1998): 591–596.

33 C. T. Robbins, C. C. Schwartz, K. A. Gunter, and C. Servheen. "Grizzly Bear Nutrition and Ecology Studies in Yellowstone National Park." *Yellowstone Science* 14(3) (2006): 19–26.

34 S. P. French and M. G. French. "Predatory Behavior of Grizzly Bears Feeding on Elk Calves in Yellowstone National Park, 1986–1988." In *Bears: Their Biology and Management*, Vol. 8, A Selection of Papers from the Eighth International Conference on Bear Research and Management, Victoria, British Columbia, Canada, February 1989 (1990), pp. 335–341.

35 K. A. Gunther, and R. Renkin. "Grizzly Bear Predation on Elk Calves and Other Fauna of Yellowstone National Park." In *Bears: Their Biology and Management*, Vol. 8, A Selection of Papers from the Eighth International Conference on Bear Research and Management, Victoria, British Columbia, Canada, February 1989, pp. 329–334.

36 F. T. van Manen, C. M. Costello, M. A. Haroldson, D. D. Bjornlie, M. R. Ebinger, K.A. Gunther, D.J. Thompson, M.D. Higgs, D. B. Tyers, S. L. Cain, K. L. Frey, B. Aber, and C. C. Schwartz. "Responses of Grizzly Bears to Changing Food Resources in the Greater Yellowstone Ecosystem." *Yellowstone Science* 23(2) (2015): 26–31.

37 M. A. Haroldson, M. A. Ternent, G. Holm, R. A. Swalley, S. Podruzny, D. Moody, and C. C. Schwartz. 1998. "Yellowstone Grizzly Bear Investigations: Annual report of the Interagency Grizzly Bear Study Team," 1997. US Geological Survey, Bozeman, Montana.

38 K. A. Gunther, M. A. Haroldson, K. Frey, S. L. Cain, J. Copeland, and C. Schwartz. 2004. "Grizzly Bear-Human Conflicts in the Greater Yellowstone Ecosystem 1992–2000." *Ursus*, Vol. 15, No. 1: 10–22.

39 Gunther, K. A. and H. E. Hoestra. "Bear-Inflicted Human Injuries in Yellowstone National Park, 1970–1994." *Ursus* 10 (1998): 377–384.

40 C. C. Schwartz and M. A. Haroldson, editors. Yellowstone grizzly bear investigations: annual report of the Interagency Grizzly Bear Study Team, 1999. US Geological Survey, Bozeman, Montana.

41 Cat Urbigkit. "WG&F Director Calls for Delisting Grizzlies from ESA." *Sublette Examiner*. January 22, 1998.

42 Cat Urbigkit. "All's Quiet on the Bear Front." *Pinedale Roundup*, August 13, 1998.

43 Cat Urbigkit. "Officials Doubt Sheepherder's Story of Grizzly Treeing." *Pinedale Roundup*. August 20, 1998.

44 Cat Urbigkit. "Grizzly Mauls Calf." *Pinedale Roundup*. Sept. 24, 1998.

45 Cat Urbigkit. "Grizzly Compensation May End." *Pinedale Roundup*. October 15, 1998.

46 Grizzly Bear-Human Conflicts, Confrontations, and Management Actions in the Yellowstone Ecosystem. 1999. Interagency Grizzly Bear Committee Yellowstone Ecosystem Subcommittee Report.

47 J. J. Craighead, J. S. Sumer, and J. A. Mitchell. *The Grizzly Bears of Yellowstone: Their Ecology in the Yellowstone Ecosystem 1959–1992.* Island Press, Washington DC: 1995.

48 M. A. Haroldson, C. C. Schwartz, S. Cherry, and D. S. Moody. "Possible effects of elk harvest on fall distribution of grizzly bears in the Greater Yellowstone Ecosystem." *Journal of Wildlife Management* 68(1) (2004).

49 Brett French. "Grizzlies and Gut Piles: Study seeks to analyze hunter-bear interactions." *Billings Gazette*, Nov. 17, 2014.

50 Brett French. "Wyoming hunter discusses bear attack." *Spokesman-Review* Nov. 3, 2013

51 C. C. Schwartz and M. A. Haroldson, editors. Yellowstone grizzly bear investigations: annual report of the Interagency Grizzly Bear Study Team 1999. US Geological Survey, Bozeman, Montana.

52 Yellowstone grizzly bear investigations: annual report of the Interagency Grizzly Bear Study Team, 2000. US Geological Survey, Bozeman, MT.

53 Yellowstone grizzly bear investigations: annual report of the Interagency Grizzly Bear Study Team, 2000. US Geological Survey, Bozeman, MT.

54 Grizzly Bear-Human Conflicts, Confrontations, and Management Actions in the Greater Yellowstone Ecosystem. Interagency Grizzly Bear Committee Yellowstone Ecosystem Subcommittee Report. Compiled by Yellowstone National Park. November 2001.

55 Ibid.

56 K. A. Gunther, M. A. Haroldson, K. Frey, S. L. Cain, J. Copeland, and C. Schwartz. "Grizzly Bear-Human Conflicts in the Greater Yellowstone Ecosystem 1992–2000." *Ursus*, Vol. 15, No. 1 (2004): 10–22.

57 Ibid.

58 (Gunther 2004 report).

59 C. C. Schwartz and M. A. Haroldson, editors. Yellowstone grizzly bear investigations: annual report of the Interagency Grizzly Bear Study Team, 2001. US Geological Survey, Bozeman, Montana.

60 Cat Urbigkit. "Managing Grizzlies." *Sublette Examiner*. April 12, 2001.

61 Cat Urbigkit. "Jim Creek grizzly dead." *Sublette Examiner*. August 9, 2001.

62 Cat Urbigkit. "No shortage of grizzlies in the Upper Green." *Sublette Examiner*. July 26, 2001.

63 Cat Urbigkit. "Forest Service Issues Thoman Grazing Violation Letter and Bridger-Teton Cites Wildlife Services for Vehicle Use." *Sublette Examiner*. September 27, 2001.

64 C. C. Schwartz and M. A. Haroldson, editors. 2001. Yellowstone grizzly bear inves-

tigations: annual report of the Interagency Grizzly Bear Study Team, 2002. US Geological Survey, Bozeman, Montana.

65 Cat Urbigkit. "Fremont County Outlaws Wolves and Grizzlies, Federal Regulation." *Sublette Examiner*. March 14, 2002.

66 Cat Urbigkit. "Sublette County Calls for Food Order to be Rescinded." *Sublette Examiner*. March 21, 2002; Cat Urbigkit. "Grizzlies, Wolves Declared "Unacceptable" in the County." *Sublette Examiner*, April 4, 2002.

67 Cat Urbigkit. "Food Storage Order Delayed." *Sublette Examiner*. March 28, 2002.

68 Cat Urbigkit. "Grizzlies, Wolves Declared "Unacceptable" in the County." *Sublette Examiner*, April 4, 2002.

69 Cat Urbigkit. "Dead Elk Remain, But Scattered." *Sublette Examiner*. June 2, 2002.

70 Cat Urbigkit. "Counties Strike Out with WG&F." *Sublette Examiner*. August 1, 2002.

71 Cat Urbigkit. "Thirteen grizzlies in Upper Green." *Sublette Examiner*. August 29, 2002.

72 Cat Urbigkit. "Grizzly Killed in Wyoming Range." *Sublette Examiner*. August 22, 2002.

73 Cat Urbigkit. "Killing Continues." *Sublette Examiner*. July 31, 2003.

74 Interagency Conservation Strategy Team. 2007. Final Conservation Strategy for the Grizzly Bear in the Greater Yellowstone Area.

75 Associated Press. "Expert Mauled by Bear was also attacked in '93." May 25, 2007.

76 Haroldson, M. A, Schwartz, C. C., and Gunther, K. A. "Grizzly Bears in the Greater Yellowstone Ecosystem." *Yellowstone Science* 16(2) (2008): 13–24.

77 Opinion. Greater Yellowstone Coalition, Inc., v. Wyoming. United States Court of Appeals for the Ninth Circuit. November 22, 2011.

78 Cat Urbigkit. "Put the scare back in the bear." *Sublette Examiner*. May 2, 2002.

79 Cat Urbigkit. "Rancher granted kill permit." *Sublette Examiner*, August 15, 2002.

80 All information about the fatal attack of Mr. Erwin Evert was taken from the July 16, 2010 Investigation Team Report: Fatality of Erwin Evert from a bear attack in Kitty Creek on the Shoshone National Forest on June 17, 2010.

81 C. C. Schwartz, M. A. Haroldson, and K. West, editors. 2010. Yellowstone grizzly bear investigations: annual report of the Interagency Grizzly Bear Study Team, 2010. US Geological Survey, Bozeman, Montana, USA.

82 Ibid.

83 All information about the Soda Butte attacks was taken from the August 13, 2010 Investigation Team Report: Attacks by a grizzly bear in Soda Butte Campground on the Gallatin National Forest on July 28, 2010.

84 C. C. Schwartz, M. A. Haroldson, and K. West, editors. 2010. Yellowstone grizzly bear investigations: annual report of the Interagency Grizzly Bear Study Team, 2010. US Geological Survey, Bozeman, Montana, USA.

85 S. M. J. G. Steyaert, C. Reusch, S. Brunberg, J. E. Swenson, K. Hacklander, and Zedrosser A. "Infanticide as a male reproductive strategy has a nutritive risk effect in brown bears." *Biology Letters* 9 (2013): 20130624.

86 S. M. J. G. Steyaert, J.E. Swenson, and A. Zedrosser. "Litter loss triggers estrus in a nonsocial seasonal breeder." *Ecology and Evolution* 4(3) (2014): 300–310.

87 S. M. J. G. Steyaert, M. Leclerc, F. Pelletier, J. Kindberg, S. Brunberg, J. E. Swenson, and A. Zedrosser. "Human shields mediate sexual conflict in a top predator". *Proceedings of the Royal Society of London B* 283 (2016): 20160906.

88 Greg Tuttle. "Retired police officer recounts bear mauling." *Billings Gazette*, July 25, 2009.

89 Martin Kidston. "Wyoming mauling victim works to help grizzlies, people coexist." *Billings Gazette*. July 9, 2012.

90 All information about the fatal attack on Brian Matayoshi was taken from the September 9, 2011 Investigation Team Report: Fatality of Mr. Brian Matayoshi from a bear attack on the Wapiti Lake Trail in Yellowstone National Park on July 6, 2011.

91 All information about the death of John Wallace was taken from the January 30, 2012 Board of Review Report: Fatality of Mr. John L. Wallace from a bear attack on the Mary Mountain Trail in Yellowstone National Park on August 25, 2011.

92 F. T. van Manen, M. A. Haroldson, D. D. Bjornlie, C. M. Costello, and M. R. Ebinger. Demographic Changes in Yellowstone's Grizzly Bear Population. *Yellowstone Science* 23(2) (2015): 17–24.

93 F. T. van Manen, M. A. Haroldson, and K. West, editors. 2011. Yellowstone grizzly bear investigations: annual report of the Interagency Grizzly Bear Study Team, 2011. US Geological Survey, Bozeman, Montana, USA.

94 M. A. Haroldson, K.A. Gunther, S.L. Cain, K.R. Wilmot, and T. Wyman. 2015. Grizzly Cub Adoptions Confirmed in Yellowstone & Grand Teton National Parks. *Yellowstone Science* 23(2): 58–61.

95 WG&F Job Completion Report 2011.

96 F.T. van Manen, M.A. Haroldson, and K. West, editors. Yellowstone grizzly bear investigations: annual report of the Interagency Grizzly Bear Study Team, 2012. US Geological Survey, Bozeman, Montana, USA.

97 WG&F Job Completion Report 2012.

98 Jennie Runevitch, WTHR. 2013. "Former Deputy Survives Grizzly Bear Attack in Wyoming." WTHR.com, Sept. 13, 2013.

99 Wyoming Grizzly Bear Job Completion Report. 2013. Wyoming Game and Fish Department, Large Carnivore Section.

100 Interagency Grizzly Bear Study Team. 2013. Response of Yellowstone grizzly bears to changes in food resources: a synthesis. Report to the Interagency Grizzly Bear Committee and Yellowstone Ecosystem Subcommittee. Interagency Grizzly Bear Study Team, US Geological Survey, Northern Rocky Mountain Science Center, Bozeman, Montana, USA.

101 F. T. van Manen, M. A. Haroldson, and S. C. Soileau, editors. Yellowstone grizzly bear investigations: Annual report of the Interagency Grizzly Bear Study Team, 2014. US Geological Survey, Bozeman, Montana, USA.

102 Craighead, Frank C. *The Track of the Grizzly*. San Francisco: Sierra Club Books, 1979.

103 Wyoming Grizzly Bear Job Completion Report. 2014. Wyoming Game and Fish Department, Large Carnivore Section.

104 Unless otherwise noted, all details of the bear attack on Adam Stewart are found in Board of Review Report—Fatality of Mr. Adam Thomas Stewart from a bear attack in Cub Creek on the Bridger-Teton National Forest on September 4, 2014, Chaired by Chris Servheen, US Fish and Wildlife Service Grizzly Bear Recovery Coordinator.

105 December 16, 2004. Recommendations of the Board of Review based on the investigation of the fatality of Mr. Adam Thomas Stewart from a bear attack in Cub Creek on the Bridger-Teton National Forest on September 4, 2014. Chaired by Chris Servheen, US Fish and Wildlife Service Grizzly Bear Recovery Coordinator.

106 K. A. Gunther and T. Wyman. Human-Habituated Bears: The Next Challenge in

Baer Management in Yellowstone National Park. *Yellowstone Science* 16(2) (2008): 35–41.

107 Louisa Willcox. "On the Death of Grizzly 760 and the Lessons of Grizzly 399's Clan." *Counterpunch*, February 26, 2015.

108 K. A. Gunther and T. Wyman. 2008. "Human-Habituated Bears: The Next Challenge in Bear Management in Yellowstone National Park." *Yellowstone Science* 16(2): 35–41.

109 Federal Register, Vol 81, No. 48, March 11, 2016. Proposed Rule, 13174–13227.

110 Interagency Grizzly Bear Study Team. 2009. Yellowstone grizzly bear mortality and conflict reduction report. Interagency Grizzly Bear Study Team, Northern Rocky Mountain Science Center, Montana State University, Bozeman, Montana, USA.

111 Federal Register, Vol. 81, No. 48, March 11, 2016. Proposed Rule, 13174–13227.

112 K. A. Gunther, K. R. Wilmot, S. L. Cain, T. Wyman, E. G. Reinertson, and A. M. Bramblett. "Habituated Grizzly Bears: A Natural Response to Increasing Visitation in Yellowstone and Grand Teton National Parks." *Yellowstone Science* 23(2) (2015): 33–39.

113 Brian DeBolt. Grizzly Bear Management Captures, Relocations, and Removals in Northwest Wyoming: 2015 Annual Report. Wyoming Game and Fish Department.

114 US Fish and Wildlife Service. Biological Opinion on US Sheep Experimental Station Grazing and Associated Projects, Agricultural Research Services. Nov. 8, 2011.

115 FWS. 2013. Report of Investigation # 2013604784R001. Sept. 30, 2015.

116 Greater Yellowstone Grizzly Bear Habitat Modeling Team. April 2015. 2014 "Grizzly Bear Annual Habitat Monitoring Report" F. T. van Manen, M. A. Haroldson, and S. C. Soileau, editors. Yellowstone grizzly bear

investigations: annual report of the Interagency Grizzly Bear Study Team, 2014. US Geological Survey, Bozeman, Montana, USA.

117 Federal Register, Vol 81, No. 48, March 11, 2016. Proposed Rule, 13174–13227.

118 Sierra Club press release dated March 3, 2016: "Sierra Club Calls For Continued Protection of Yellowstone Grizzly Bears."

119 Press release: "US Fish and Wildlife Service Proposes to Prematurely Delist Greater Yellowstone Area Grizzly Bears from the Endangered Species Act." March 3, 2016.

120 Email: Center for Biological Diversity, Breaking: Feds Walk Away From Yellowstone's Grizzlies, March 4, 2016.

121 Sylvia Fallon's Blog, Switchboard. Natural Resources Defense Council Staff Blog. March 3, 2016.

122 Wyoming Wildlife Advocates, "USFWS Proposes Delisting Yellowstone Ecosystem Grizzlies From Endangered Species Act Protections." Press release, March 3, 2016.

123 H. Forsgren, and S. Talbott. Viewpoint: Management Key to Grizzly Recovery. *Ravalli Republic*, Dec. 15, 2012.

124 Wayne Pacelle. "The Brewing Battle Over Grizzly Delisting and Trophy Hunting in the Yellowstone Ecosystem." *A Humane Nation Blog*, January 5, 2016.

125 David Mattson. Declaration of David Mattson. December 22, 2014.

126 *Grizzly Times*. Accessed March 22, 2016: http://www.grizzlytimes.org/#!debunking-delisting/cxv6.

127 Louisa Willcox. "Don't Delist and Risk Yellowstone Grizzly Bears' Future." *Counterpunch*, March 11, 2016: http://www.counterpunch.org/2016/03/11/dont-delist-and-risk-yellowstone-grizzly-bears-future/.

128 Mattson, David. "Disserving the Public Trust: The Despotic Future of Grizzly Bear Management." *Counterpunch*. May 20, 2016.

129 The Humane Society of the United States. April 12, 2016: American Voters Oppose Delisting Greater Yellowstone Area Grizzly Bears from Endangered Species Act Protections.

130 Stephen Herrero. *Bear Attacks: Their Causes and Avoidance.* New York: Lyons Press, 2002.

131 Conservation Strategy. 2016.

132 Mike Koshmrl. "What Happens when Hunters and Grizzlies Collide?" *Jackson Hole News and Guide.* October 7, 2015.

133 A. T. Morehouse, T. A. Graves, N. Mikle, and M. S. Boyce. "Nature vs. Nurture: Evidence for Social Learning of Conflict Behavior in Grizzly Bears." *PLOS ONE* 11(11) (2016): e0165425.

134 Ibid.

135 Thompson, Dan. March 7, 2017. Grizzly Bear Management in Wyoming. Wyoming Game and Fish Commission meeting, Riverton, Wyoming.

136 2017 Known and Probable Grizzly Bear Mortalities in the Greater Yellowstone Ecosystem. Interagency Grizzly Bear Study Team.

137 82 *Federal Register* R 30502, June 30, 2017; RIN 1018–BA41, Endangered and Threatened Wildlife and Plants; Removing the Greater Yellowstone Ecosystem Population of Grizzly Bears From the Federal List of Endangered and Threatened Wildlife.

138 Buckrail. "She's back: Grand Griz 399 wakes with cubs in Grand Teton National Park." May 4, 2018.

139 Matthew Brown, Associated Press. "Grizzly researcher in 'dream job' attacked by bear." *Missoulian.* May 24, 2018.

140 Zac Taylor. "Griz killed: Self-defense claimed in shooting of bear." *Cody Enterprise.* May 23, 2018.

141 US Fish and Wildlife Service. Grizzly Bear 5-Year Review: Summary and Evaluation. 2011. FWS Grizzly Bear Recovery Office, Missoula, MT.

142 D. D. Bjornlie, M. A. Haroldson, D. J. Thompson, C. C. Schwartz, K. A. Gunther, S.L. Cain, D. B. Tyers, K. L. Frey. "Expansion of Occupied Grizzly Bear Range." *Yellowstone Science* 23(2) (2015): 54–57.